T0163591

ONE STEP AT A TIME

ONE STEP at a TIME

OUR MISSIONARY PILGRIMAGE

Elmer & Eileen
LEHMAN

NASHVILLE

LONDON • NEW YORK • MELBOURNE • VANCOUVER

ONE STEP AT A TIME
Our Missionary Pilgrimage

Published in New York, New York, by Morgan James Publishing. Morgan James is a trademark of Morgan James, LLC. www.MorganJamesPublishing.com

The Morgan James Speakers Group can bring authors to your live event. For more information or to book an event visit The Morgan James Speakers Group at www.TheMorganJamesSpeakersGroup.com.

ISBN 9781683508953 paperback
ISBN 9781683508960 eBook
Library of Congress Control Number: 2017918799

Cover Design by:
Rachel Lopez
www.r2cdesign.com

Interior Design by:
Christopher Kirk
www.GFSstudio.com

In an effort to support local communities, raise awareness and funds, Morgan James Publishing donates a percentage of all book sales for the life of each book to Habitat for Humanity Peninsula and Greater Williamsburg.

Get involved today! Visit
www.MorganJamesBuilds.com

COSTA RICA

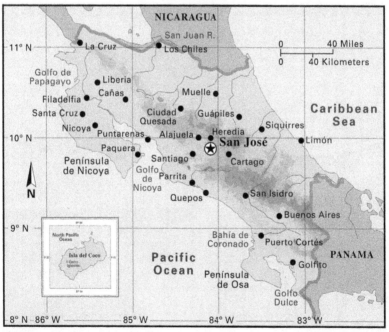

Printed by Impresión Comercial. La Nación S.A.

FOREWORD

Not for us, but for Him.

That sums up the heart of Elmer and Eileen Lehman's missionary pilgrimage. You could say this phrase represents the story of their lives. With much prayer and a little persuasion, they decided to pen this journey so that the calling on their lives might encourage others to know that God is faithful to those who obey the call. The call is not always convenient, and true servants never feel qualified. God has a way of calling His people into responsibilities far too great for them, but never too great for Him.

Elmer dropped out of high school after his sophomore year to help out on his family's dairy farm. Eileen, as a farm girl, enjoyed her studies and was encouraged by her mother to pursue a teaching career in elementary education. She interrupted this career once she married Elmer in 1953 and they settled down in a mobile home on his father's dairy farm.

God does not wait for His people to get a degree or a title behind their name to do the one thing required of us, and that is to hear and follow His plan for our lives. As we pray and seek the Lord, step by step and day by day, opportunity after opportunity comes. So, for more than 60 years, that is what they have done. Prayed and sought. Sought and prayed.

Elmer and Eileen's prayer was that with the telling of this journey, a young missionary family might be encouraged. A seasoned believer might be ready to respond to that God-given call, forsaking the mere pursuit of worldly possessions, taking up their cross and following Christ. They pray other fellow missionaries will be spurred to share their testimonies as well.

There is truly nothing new under the sun and while someone reading this may be seeking God's plan for his or her life, Elmer and Eileen hope that you know they can relate. They want to encourage you to pray until you hear from God and do not doubt what He tells you to do. Trust in your ability to hear the voice of the Lord through the working of the Holy Spirit.

They want to leave you with the scripture that meant so much to them as they began their journey, carrying them through the more than 60 years of their marriage, and all of their missionary journeys: from northern New York State to Puerto Rico; back to the states for study in Harrisonburg, Virginia; from there to Costa Rica; and back to America to Rosedale and Hilliard, Ohio.

"You are my portion, O Lord; I have promised to obey your words." Psalm 119:57.

April Barker
Founder and CEO of Dream Builder for Empire of Dreams, LLC

TABLE OF CONTENTS

THE FORMATIVE YEARS

Elmer

My parents were married in 1923 and the next year my father purchased the home farm from his father. This was in northern New York State where dairy cows provided the major source of income. Dad and Mom raised eight children. After two sons, they had a daughter, but she only lived 2 ½ months. Then they had a third son, followed by another daughter. I was next as child number five, and I sometimes wondered if this was a disappointment to them to now have four sons but only one daughter. But, God was good to them. The final children were all three daughters, so our parents raised four sons and four daughters. All of us were approximately two years apart in age.

They named me Elmer Junior, and I grew up being called Junior. When I became a young man, my wife-to-be was able to get people to call me Elmer. I was born on June 28, 1931, which was right in the middle of what was known as the Great Depression. It was a difficult time financially, but I never heard my parents complain about their large family. You could say that we were poor, but we did not know it; so we were happy.

There were always plenty of jobs for children to do on the farm, and we were a hard-working family. The farm developed into what, at that time, was a large operation with about fifty milk cows, plus another twenty heifers and calves, plus two teams of workhorses. When the time came to start school, we walked three quarters of a mile to the local elementary one room school. There was one teacher for approximately 25 students in grades one to six. There was no kindergarten. After first grade, there was a teacher change and I had the same teacher for the next five years. A music teacher came around one day a week, and she taught me to love to sing. I sang alto, and on one occasion, I was really putting my all into it, and soon the entire class was singing alto with me.

That walk to and from school through the northern New York winters was often made with cold feet, but it seemed the normal thing to do at the time. After sixth grade, we transferred to the local high school where grades seven to twelve were taught. We continued to walk to and from the local elementary school, where we traveled by bus to the high school. Eventually, the bus routes were changed and we boarded the bus in front of our house. But, we were some of the first ones to board the bus in the morning, so even that could be a cold ride until the bus gradually warmed up.

The school arrangement was now much different, as we had a homeroom teacher and a different teacher for each class. There were about 25 students in the class. Several of them were my peers at church as well. Our family was not involved in any after-school sports, but went directly home on the bus and quickly changed into work clothes to help out on the farm.

The long summer evenings did give us enough daylight to get together with neighbor children for a ball game, or to go swimming in the creek that flowed through our farm and served as the neighborhood swimming hole. The rolling hills on the farm were good for sledding in the winter, and the pond behind the barn was good for ice skating. We also cut ice for the neighbors, and for ourselves, to store in icehouses where the ice, packed in sawdust, would be used to cool the milk during the summer months.

As I finished my sophomore year of high school, and approached age 16, school attendance was no longer compulsory. Dad asked me how interested I was in finishing high school and let me know he could really use me on the farm. He, himself, had not gone beyond sixth grade, although he was an avid reader, and could skim through a book in one evening and remember its content. I expected to be a farmer all my life and finishing high school did not seem that important. So, I dropped out to help where I was needed on the family farm.

Church life was important. As a family, we attended church and Sunday school regularly as well as service on Sunday evenings, and on other special occasions. Family devotions, with daily scripture reading and prayer, following breakfast were part of our routine.

My younger sisters and I would often play church in the room set aside as a playroom above the kitchen. They would play with their dolls that sometimes behaved and sometimes did not. I was the preacher. One day I was expounding on the Sermon on the Mount when my father decided to come in, sit down, and listen to me preach. I immediately became too embarrassed to continue. He begged me to keep on but I refused. That changed later in life when on several occasions I was preaching in a local church. He would follow me around to listen to me. I was no longer playing church. I was then trying to help the church to be the church.

An unfortunate experience developed in the church when I was ten years old. The church was quite strict regarding dress standards and a discord developed when a group of persons begged for a loosening of the standards and others wanted to maintain the standards as they were. The differences could not be reconciled, families were divided and a division occurred in the congregation. Attitudes and verbal expressions were far from those appropriate to professing Christians. As often happens in times like these, the issues that seemed so important at the time became non-issues a generation later, and the two congregations developed a good relationship. But for me as a ten-year-old boy, I could have become bitter and turned off by the church. Thankfully, God did not let that happen. My parents were torn between the two groups and finally, they decided to unite with the group more open to change. But, they personally maintained the dress standards required by the more conservative group. They allowed us, as children, to choose whichever congregation we preferred.

When I was fifteen years old, I found that a number of my peers decided to be baptized and affiliate with the church. It seemed like the right time for me, so I talked with my mother about baptism. There was no dramatic or crisis conversion experience, but yes, a sincere and genuine desire to follow Christ in life. With my parents' blessing, I entered the baptismal class at the more conservative of the two churches. The church had its traditions, which included a rather large baptismal class each year. There were approximately eighteen of us. Each Sunday morning we filed in to the front row, always in the same order: fellows on one side; and girls on the other. Each Sunday morning before the sermon one of the pastors would give a pre-sermon talk geared toward this group preparing for baptism.

As a Mennonite denomination, we had a Mennonite Confession of Faith, which clearly explained what we, as a church, believed. Interestingly, this document was written in 1632 in Holland, translated into English, and carried down through the centuries. One written in 1963 finally replaced it, which was again replaced in 1995. We were each asked to memorize one of the articles from this 1632 Confession, and since I was number six in the group, I memorized Article Six, which was "Repentance and Amendment of Life." On the Sunday before baptism, we were asked to give this memorized article in public, and on August 31, 1947, we were baptized. I was sixteen.

Is this the way it should be done? God is not as concerned about our methods as He is about our commitment. In those days our pastors were chosen right out of the congregation, and they were untrained, but self-educated men, highly committed to the Lord and the church. One of them was recognized as the bishop, who was really the senior pastor, two were associate pastors, and one was a deacon. All were bi-vocational with their own means of livelihood. Each of these leaders was assigned to a group of the candidates preparing for baptism.

The deacon came to visit me. Among the questions he asked regarding my commitment and understanding of the Christian faith, was the final question when he asked if it was my sincere desire to follow Jesus and His will for my life. I answered with a definite "Yes, it is." I knew it was a serious commitment. As I reflect on that large group of persons baptized that day, a few of them have passed on to their eternal reward. To my knowledge, every one of the rest of the group is active in the church today and faithfully following Jesus. God was able to use this method, as we promised to obey His words.

My parents had the joy of seeing each of their children commit their lives to Jesus. Four out of the eight have now passed on to their eternal reward. The four of us who are left continue with our hope in God, Who is our portion.

Eileen

On January 6, 1933 my mother wrote in her diary, "Stella and the doctor came this morning about 3 o'clock. At about 6 our baby girl was born 8 lbs." Our neighbor, Stella Rowsam was from the farm next to ours. On January 10 my mother recorded, "We named the baby Eileen Fanny today."

I was the first daughter and was welcomed by two brothers, Floyd and Walter. As I grew up, I became more appreciative of them. We did a lot of things together. They taught me how to drive the truck in the hay field at a time that hay was loaded onto a truck or wagon in the field.

Eight more children followed me, so we became a total of eleven siblings: six girls and five boys. Our parents made each of us feel special and wanted. On one occasion, a neighbor lady stopped by to see my mother. Mother was doing something special. She was in the process of making doll clothes for our dolls. The lady looked directly at us and said, "Girls, you have a real mother!"

My elementary education began in a one-room country school in West Martinsburg in northern New York State. My two older brothers were already enrolled. I appreciated the support they gave me. My oldest brother was quite protective of us younger ones. In the community where our school was located, we had a struggle with some of our schoolmates who teased us regularly because of our church habits, calling us names and ridiculing us.

Our school was located one and a half miles from our home. In the wintertime it made for a cold walk and we had cold toes by the time we arrived at school. Our teacher would allow us to sit near the stove to thaw out. My father would often haul cans of fresh milk to the drop off at the station in town. This would allow us children to get a ride on our way to school.

Our school changed teachers nearly every year, which made it difficult for teachers and students to maintain stability. When I arrived in the upper grades we were rewarded with a wonderful teacher who saw potential in the students and encouraged us to do our best. She encouraged me to compete at a spelling bee at the county fair. I was too shy.

This was a time of centralization in which one or two-room schools were closed in favor of busing students to a nearby town with buildings adequate to accommodate the whole school population. The centralization was a big adjustment for rural students who now depended on using public transportation.

After school I knew what was expected of me. My job awaiting me was to peel the potatoes for the evening meal—supper. There were other jobs, too. During "sugaring season" all of us had extra chores. The operation for boiling sap into maple syrup was a distance from our farm and the men of the family would spend hours there during this season. We would return from school, change our clothes, go out to the barn and throw silage from the silo to feed the cows. By doing this work, we were able to help to alleviate the evening chores of the men of the family.

Annual revival meetings were held in our church and our family took them seriously. I was around the age of 12 and I remember those meetings clearly. One evening the preacher chose to speak from a text in the Old Testament, having to do with the death of Absalom and King David's query concerning him. He asked, "Is the young man safe? Is the young woman safe?" The Holy Spirit convicted me that evening and I responded by standing to my feet.

The next morning I went downstairs for breakfast and my mother congratulated and encouraged me. After the meeting several of us were encouraged to meet for Instruction, in preparation for baptism. This was a small class, which met during Sunday school and climaxed in our being baptized. In attending a Christian high school for my senior year, I realized how blessed I was to have received a wonderful Christian orientation as a single woman.

During summer vacation we would sometimes fix up a room on the back stairs of the big farmhouse. We actually enjoyed playing school and teaching lessons such as spelling. We also had an active Science Club. I was already honing my teaching skills and enjoying it.

When I was 10 years old, a dramatic change came to our family. There was to be an ordination to the Christian ministry of a brother from our congregation. The mystery surrounding this was that no one knew who that brother would be. In preparation, members were encouraged to submit names from the congregation of possible candidates for ministry.

Sunday evening came, and with it, a heightened anxiousness. The men who had been selected sat at the front of the church. A paper had been placed in one of several hymnbooks on a table close to the men who had been selected. The men were invited to choose a book, which each felt moved to select. The presiding minister then looked into the books to see which one had the paper. It happened that my dad had chosen the book with the indicated paper in it. The words on the paper were from Proverbs 16:33: "The lot is cast into the lap but the whole disposing thereof is of the Lord."

This was a sacred moment and an emotional one for my parents. At the time we children did not fully understand, but we quickly adjusted to the change of having our Dad as a minister. As his sons grew older, they were able to do much of the farm work, giving our Dad more time to the ministry.

During the same service, my Grandpa Zehr, my dad's father, was ordained as bishop. He and Grandma came to our house many times to share with our parents. My dad took his calling very seriously and counted on us to pray for him. But, he, as well as my mother, also gave quality time to us children, and all eleven now live committed lives to the Lord. One son, and his wife and three of their daughters, as well as their husbands, became involved in pastoral leadership responsibilities, with two of the couples serving for several years in overseas mission assignments. Several of the children became involved in teaching roles, or in the medical profession. All of us speak highly and fondly of the parents God gave us.

Lehman Homestead, Lowville, New York.

Zehr Homestead, Lowville, New York.

Chapter 1

EACH FOR THE OTHER, AND BOTH FOR GOD

Elmer

Three major decisions face all of us early in life. Do I commit to Jesus as Savior and Lord? If I marry, who is the one for me? What is God leading me to do in life?

Eileen and I both had similar backgrounds of growing up on dairy farms. We had a similar church background. Our families had known each other for many years. Our educational backgrounds were quite different, with me dropping out of high school to help on the farm, and Eileen graduating from a Christian high school in Virginia and taking a year of college. We were both interested in Bible study and a committed Christian life. After Eileen's first year of college, she stayed home to care for her baby sister, almost 18 years younger than she, and while Eileen's sister next to her attended that same high school in Virginia for her senior year.

I had the opportunity to attend a winter Bible Institute in Kitchener, Ontario for a six-week term, and then return home to help on the farm. Both of us had been away and met some fine young people from other communities, but our hearts were drawn to establish relationships within our home community. Our congregation was composed of approximately 500 active members and had two meeting places with Sunday morning services at both places. The Sunday evening services alternated between the two places. Eileen was in the Lowville congregation and I was in the Croghan congregation, but we were aware of each other. The young people all met together in one group. Eileen found ways to continue her preparation for a teaching career, and enrolled in an extension course from Potsdam State Teachers College in northern New York State, which was taught one night weekly at her local high school.

Eileen was not aware that for several weeks I had been watching her and looking for an opportunity to begin a courtship. I was 19 and she would soon be turning 18. The opportunity came on Christmas Eve, 1950. I befriended a young man who was dating Eileen's sister at the time. We decided to arrange a double date for that evening. Since it was a Sunday evening, we were at the regular evening service, and then the young people, as was traditional on Christmas Eve, divided into groups to go out and carol for the elderly and shut-ins from the congregation.

When my friend made contact with Eileen's sister, Eileen was with her, and I seized the opportunity. God had opened the door. She seemed pleasantly surprised, but also grateful for the opportunity. Each of us knew of the other's total commitment to the Lordship of Christ, with the kind of qualities one looks for in a Christian partner. So, the four of us crowded into the 1949 Chevrolet pickup that belonged to my dad, and off we went with five more young people who were in another auto-mobile. It was a cold winter evening, but we just enjoyed being together. We would hop out and sing about three Christmas hymns standing outside a window, and then jump back in the vehicle to warm up, and go on to the next house.

One of the elderly was Eileen's maternal grandmother. She was excited to see Eileen standing outside singing, and I was standing right beside her. Our date was soon family knowl-edge. We were serious about courtship and were not interested in casual dating. From the beginning, we anticipated that this would be a long-term relationship and it continued that way. Friends and family members affirmed our relationship as one where we were right for each other. Eileen's siblings definitely encouraged her. In marriage, we do not only marry the individ-ual, but we marry into a family.

One week after that first date, I again attended a six-week term at Ontario Mennonite Bible Institute. I enjoyed the in-depth Bible study and the opportunity to exercise my musi-cal talent in a men's quartet.

Although we were not aware of it at the time, it was the beginning of carrying out a courtship largely by correspon-dence. We wrote letters a number of times during those six weeks, and this was just the beginning. After I returned to the farm, we saw each other regularly, and this was enhanced by another development. A few days after our first date, we dis-covered that the two of us had been named to a committee of four to plan activities for our young people. These activi-ties would bring about 100 young people together, so it was quite a challenge. We would plan a variety of programs from serious appropriate themes to humorous skits and wholesome entertainment. The youth responded well. It was a delight to sit together in these committee meetings, and then follow with quality time for the two of us.

An opportunity came for Eileen to get a teaching job in a local rural, one-room school. Each school had its own local Board of Directors, and the lady who interviewed Eileen was delighted with what she saw. But then, the Powers-That-Be let her know that they were not to hire a teacher who did not yet have her degree. Soon, another opportunity came, and this was to teach in a private Christian school, grades 1-4, in a two-room school called Alden Christian School, located about twenty miles east of Buffalo in western New York, and 200 miles away from her home. To better prepare, she would take summer school at Eastern Mennonite College in Virginia. This meant seeking to keep our courtship strong, while not seeing much of each other. There were no computers so no one had ever heard of email or Facebook. Nor were there cell phones or texting. Long distance calls were a luxury, so that was not an option. Fourteen miles separated our two homes and phone calls were long distance, at 17 cents for a three-minute call. So, why not just write a letter, even when both were at home? I recall the occasion when Eileen wanted to invite me to come to her house for the Sunday noon meal. She invited me by letter, rather than make a phone call.

Every Sunday evening after church, young men would take their girlfriends home from church on their weekly date. I would go home and write a letter to my most special friend, and mail it the next day with a three-cent stamp. Eileen would do the same. As time went on, it increased to twice a week, and sometimes even more often.

When I reached the age of 21, my parents recognized that I was now on my own. They gave me a $500 gift, and my father employed me with a salary. My parents would give me room and board, gasoline for my car, and a salary of $150 monthly for eight months, and $125 monthly for the four slower winter months, for an annual salary of $1700. My father helped me locate a car and he financed it. It was the personal car of the local Chevrolet dealer, and was a one-year-old 1951 four-door sedan, with 10,000 miles of use. New cars cost about $2,000, and the dealer sold this one to us for $1,675. I put the $500 from my parents toward this purchase, and collected money from my salary only as I needed it, putting the rest toward the loan. I repaid my father in less than a year.

I was involved with Eileen's brothers and a number of other young men in the congregation in a tract distribution ministry in urban areas. We began a program of erecting gospel signs along several main highways in the county, with a plan to rotate the signs on a regular basis. We were also involved in monthly meetings at the county jail, and in services in retirement homes. All of this gave me the opportunity to visit Eileen's home regularly, even when she was not there. I was always well received by her family.

One of the gospel signs read "After death, what then?" It was based on Hebrews 9:27, and was placed on one corner of the farm of my father, along a state highway. One night a young man from the congregation was riding his motorcycle when he was struck by a speeding automobile. The young man's lifeless body was hurled up against the foot of that sign. Eileen's father preached his funeral sermon, using Hebrews 9:27 as a text. "It is appointed unto men once to die, but after this the judgment." It was a sobering time for the congregation.

Eileen's parents arranged for her to come home about one weekend a month, returning home on Friday evening and going back to her job on Sunday afternoon. She came home for the summer, but that was again interrupted by taking summer school in Virginia and returning to western New York State for another school year. But then, another development took place.

In the summer of 1952 my older brother was married in Ohio. I invited Eileen and my younger sister invited her boy-friend to join the family for the wedding. We returned home, and a few days later, Eileen would be leaving again for another school year. The event was not in the planning for a long time, although I was convinced Eileen was the person I wanted to be with as long as life should last. So, before saying goodnight and good-bye for a lengthy period, I decided to pop the ques-tion. Naturally, there was a warm embrace and an affectionate kiss. There was then a special time of prayer in committing our lives to the Lord to serve Him together, and keep Christ central in our marriage. This was not our first experience of praying together by any means, but it was a most special experience. Our engagement was our secret. We told no one from that time of commitment in August 1952 until the following Valentine's Day, when we made the announcement public. Since in our conservative religious background, engagement rings were con-sidered as ornamental jewelry, I bought Eileen a wristwatch. Times have changed since then.

The engagement announcement included our photo and the words from the Book of Ruth in the King James Ver-sion. "Whither thou goest, I will go; where thou lodgest I will lodge; thy people shall be my people and thy God my God." It then built on the letter E with "Eileen" horizontally and "Elmer" vertically, and "ENGAGED" diagonally, all tied to the same letter E.

Several weeks before our wedding, we began helping out at a church planting location in a rural community called Pine Grove. Eileen's father was one of the early visionaries who helped get this church started. It began with Vacation Bible School with Eileen's father as superintendent and Eileen as one of the teachers. When regular Sunday services began, both of us taught Sunday school classes and I helped out as worship leader, where hymns were sung without accompaniment. From our experience there, we gathered ideas that were good to put into practice, as well as what mistakes should be avoided, as we later entered into our own church-planting assignment.

From our first date until our wedding day, two years and eight months had passed. I was now 22 and Eileen was 20. Wedding plans had to be made largely by correspondence. Eileen's father, as a pastor, would perform the ceremony at the Lowville Mennonite Church on a Saturday forenoon. Weather permitting, a reception would be held on the lawn at the home of Eileen's parents. Relatives, especially the sisters of the mothers of the bride and groom, would work together to prepare the noon meal. It turned out to be a beautiful, sunny day. We chose Saturday August 29, 1953 as our special day.

We planned a two-week honeymoon, spending the first week in the mountains of New England, with four nights in a cabin with cooking facilities in New Hampshire, and then the second week we visited friends in Pennsylvania and western

New York State. The entire honeymoon cost about $125, with motel costs averaging about five dollars a night.

Even before our marriage, we discussed our desire to give two years to the church's program called Voluntary Service, where one received room and board and a small stipend of spending money each month. We discussed how we would enjoy working in a children's home. But, when would that opportunity come? The wisest decision seemed to be to settle on my father's farm. He had purchased a used 8 X 33 feet mobile home, which would become our home to begin our marriage and to see what the Lord's next steps would be for us. We both sensed that something more was on the horizon. What would it be? We would wait on the Lord and see.

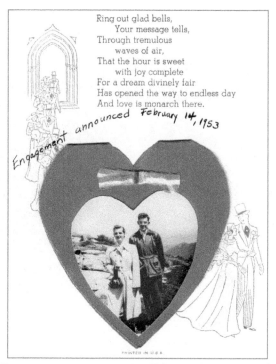

Our engagement announcement February 1953, six months
before our wedding.

Our first home, destroyed by fire on January 1, 1954, four
months into our marriage.

Chapter 2
THE TURNING POINT

Eileen

Making wedding plans by correspondence was not simple. We would see each other approximately one weekend a month and that was helpful. But, there would be adjustments. I enjoyed my teaching career and was excited about teaching another year. I was actively involved in the activities of the Alden Mennonite Church in the community where I was now living.

Should Elmer leave the farm and get a job in western New York State so we could be together? Should we wait another year to get married? I could even get excited about going back to college and getting my degree.

Elmer was also actively involved in the activities and the ministries of our church in northern New York State. He had again been chosen to be a part of the planning committee of the youth activities, after being off the committee for one year. In addition, His father needed him on the family farm.

As the time came to set a wedding date, we both knew we did not want any more lengthy separations. We decided we were not willing to wait any longer, so we proceeded with plans for an August 29 wedding date. After a two-week honeymoon to Vermont, New Hampshire, eastern Pennsylvania and western New York, we settled into the mobile home on the farm of Elmer's parents. Further education and teaching for me would need to wait.

Elmer and I got involved in the church planting ministry at Pine Grove and in the outreach ministries of the Croghan and Lowville congregations. Some of Elmer's active involvement included a male quartet and the local choir called "Mennonite Youth Chorus," as well as working on the youth committee. Although now married, he continued in this role until the expiration of his term at the end of the year.

Elmer kept busy working on the farm, and I picked up jobs wherever I could, much of it was housecleaning for local people. That was quite a change from teaching, but it was what was available at the time. I enrolled in a correspondence course from Penn State University as one more step toward a college degree.

We had not given up on our desire to go into the voluntary service program of the church, but continued to wait on the Lord for the appointed time. Even before our marriage, we had discussed how we would enjoy working in a children's home. Four months passed rather uneventfully, and on New Year's Eve, the youth gathered for a special evening to receive the New Year. We spent time in prayer, especially seeking to know and do God's will in our lives. There was no way of knowing what the Lord would allow us to go through the next day—our first New Year together.

We woke up New Year's Day to a bitterly cold winter day. Although, in setting up the mobile home, we had packed the water line into a section of stove pipe packed in sawdust for insulation, it was not enough to keep the water from freezing. Elmer's parents and younger sisters were invited to the home of his older sister and family for New Year's Day, but we decided to stay home and try to unfreeze the water line. Elmer plugged in a heat lamp to warm it up, but at noon the line was still frozen, so he unplugged the lamp and we sat down to eat together.

While eating, I observed that the water line had opened up. But soon, I saw smoke coming through the tile on the floor. Elmer quickly rushed outside and saw that the entire under-side of the mobile home was burning. We could not imagine that a heat lamp would create enough heat to ignite the saw-dust, but it did.

Elmer rushed into the farmhouse to call the volunteer fire department, but the phone was not working. We jumped into our car and speeded to the village one and a half miles away. We knew there was a siren in front of the fire department, and Elmer pulled the lever to set it off. Someone quickly came and Elmer told him where the fire was. We rushed back home, and by then, the fire was creeping up the walls of the building beside the mobile home, which was old and used as a hen house. At the time it was empty, with the exception of three fatted hogs in the basement level. The fire had grown and there was no way to get back into the mobile home to save anything.

It was amazing how quickly volunteer firemen were able to drop what they were doing, and get to the fire. The pond behind the barn served as a valuable source of water after chopping a hole through the ice. Two more volunteer fire departments were called but the mobile home, the hen house and the garage next to it, were all destroyed. The firemen were able to pull the three fattened hogs to safety through the basement window. They were also able to protect the four-stall garage just across the driveway.

We were left with the clothes on our backs and a three-year-old vehicle. Everything else was gone. This included our clothing, our wedding gifts, our wedding pictures, and photos from our honeymoon. I had two more lessons completed from my correspondence course and ready to mail when they were consumed by the fire. My brother encouraged me to write to my professor and explain the situation. My professor was understanding and kindly sent me a new textbook and gave me extended time to redo the lessons and send them to him.

The day after the fire was Sunday. Elmer got out of his farm clothes and into dress clothes and shoes that his father and his brother-in-law had loaned to him. His Dad was a large man so his shoes were too big, but that was better than going barefoot. I also borrowed clothing from my family. The next week we went out to buy clothing and I invested in a sewing machine and used my sewing skills to make dresses for myself. The youth from our "Mennonite Youth Chorus" gave us funds for Elmer to buy a new suit.

As we reflected on this sad experience, we sought to discern what the Lord was trying to tell us. He seemed to be saying, "You have nothing left here. Now is the time to go." We talked with Elmer's parents, and although it was not easy for them to accept that after raising four sons, his father would now need to go out and hire someone to assist on the farm. They tried to understand and did not want to stand in the way of what we felt God was leading us to do.

We applied to what was then known as Mennonite Board of Missions (now Mennonite Mission Network) in Elkhart, Indiana, to see what openings there might be for voluntary service. There was an option of working among Native Americans, who were migrant workers in the Southwest, but the personnel at the office were not convinced that this was the best use of our gifts. They encouraged us to wait a few months and see what opportunities might become available. It was not easy to wait. The Psalmist says, "Wait for the Lord; be strong and take heart and wait for the Lord." Psalm 27:14. God is not in a hurry but He is always on time.

Elmer's parents fixed up temporary living quarters upstairs in their home. That playroom where Elmer used to "preach" as a child was now our kitchen and we shared the family bathroom. We settled in and waited.

Then it happened. One July day Elmer was working in the hayfield when I walked out with a letter from Elkhart. The Missions office had received a letter from a children's home in Puerto Rico, asking if the Mission would have a couple that could be available as soon as possible to administer the home. It was a home for undernourished children who would come for three months or more to receive good nourishment. There were ten acres of land, a couple of cows, some hens, and rabbits. They wanted to know if a couple would be available where the husband had farming experience and the wife had teaching experience? The letter stated, "We believe you are that couple."

It excited us, but it also scared us. "They speak that strange-sounding Spanish language there don't they?" "How could we ever learn that?" "What do we know about administering a children's home?" These are the questions we asked. We had always been employees. But again, the Lord was showing us that assignments that were too big for us were not too big for Him.

The next several weeks were filled with preparations, further communication with the Missions office, and Elmer's father lining up hired help to replace him on the farm. The home congregation had a farewell service for us on August 29, 1954—our first wedding anniversary. September 7, 1954 came, and with it some difficult farewells. Then we boarded the train in Utica, New York to travel to Elkhart, Indiana, riding through the night. It was Elmer's first train ride and my second. After three days of orientation, we again, boarded a train to continue on to Chicago, taxied to the airport, and had our first plane ride to Miami and on to San Juan, Puerto Rico.

We were met by people we did not know and had a three-hour ride around hills and curves to the interior village of La Plata, which would be our home for six weeks for language study, and preparation for our assignment. We were in a strange land, hearing a strange language, adapting to a strange culture, getting acclimatized to the tropical climate. We were no longer living in our own familiar home but in a community. But we were assured that God brought us out of our comfort zone and had placed us here as the next step in His plan for our lives. What would come next? He had shown us His plan for the next two years, and we trusted Him for our future. His eternal Word continues to speak. Jeremiah 29:11: "I know the plans I have for you, declares the Lord, plans to prosper you and not to harm you, plans to give you hope and a future."

That was a sad day when we stood there and watched that cruel fire consume what we had worked so hard to accomplish. But God was able to use this sad event to open a beautiful door to take us another step closer to what He still had waiting for us. His plan is always best.

Chapter 3

THE ISLE OF ENCHANTMENT

Elmer

O ur travels from our home community in northern New York State had taken us as far south as the state of Virginia, as far west as Indiana, as far east as New Hampshire, and as far north as southern Ontario, Canada. We had now travelled as far as Chicago, then by plane to Miami and San Juan, Puerto Rico, to spend the next two years on this beautiful tropical island, known as the Isle of Enchantment.

Our flight left Chicago in the night at 12:30 A.M., and we left Miami at 8:30 in the morning. Our air tickets cost $93.30 per person. We made our way inland that afternoon to La Plata, which would be our home for six weeks of language study. We were fascinated by all the strange sights. Men were plowing the hillsides with oxen. Women were doing their laundry in local streams. Small huts, often without electricity and running water, filled the landscape. Animals roamed loose on the highway. Flowering trees added to the luscious, tropical growth.

When Christopher Columbus returned to Spain in 1493, after his second trip to the Americas and his discovery of Puerto Rico, as the story goes, the queen asked him what Puerto Rico was like. He took a sheet of paper, wrinkled it into a ball, and threw it on a table, saying, "That's it." Although somewhat exaggerated, it is true that it is an island of mountains, valleys, hills, and curves. We saw highways with as many as thirty curves in a one-mile stretch.

This little island, 35 miles wide and 100 miles long, was home to two million people. Today the population is almost twice as large, with more Puerto Ricans residing in the continental United States, than living in Puerto Rico.

After six weeks of language study, we moved five miles away to Aibonito to the children's home called "Casa de Salud" (House of Health). We were quickly thrust into carrying out our responsibilities. The Board of Directors of well-to-do citizens of the island, both Protestant and Catholic, managed the home. Their purpose was to provide a home for undernourished children, almost always living below poverty level, who would usually come for a period of three months, although occasionally for six months, and in a couple of cases, for nine months or a year. Our job was to "fatten them up." We took each child's picture when he or she arrived, and weighed each one every week.

Some of the children had eaten dirt. Others had eaten soap. Some would throw stones at other children. Some of the children were unwanted but most of them were hungry for love. Social workers, welfare agencies, and school principals referred them to us.

The staff at the home was composed of ten to twelve people, working as house parents, cooks, a laundrywoman, maintenance men, and a farmer. The Board of Directors called me the Administrator and Eileen the Director.

The majority of the children came from Catholic homes and would walk to the local Catholic Church each Sunday with their housemothers. We were permitted to take the several Protestant children in the home to church with us to the La Plata Mennonite Church, five miles away. The church provided a vehicle to haul the children, and I drove it. Some of the Catholic children begged to go with us so they could ride to church, but we were careful to respect the wishes of the parents. We were able to instill wholesome habits and proper behavior in the children's lives, and were able to be open in sharing our testimony with the members of the staff. We knew that they observed us closely, and they felt free to come to us with questions about our beliefs. We had the joy of seeing one of our employees, a young man named Miguel, commit his life to Christ.

In the early weeks, it was a challenge to answer the phone in Spanish. We joked about speaking in signs and wonders, which meant trying to use signs as we spoke so people would understand us, with the hearer wondering what we meant. But, talking with signs was not helpful on the phone. As the only North Americans in the home, we learned Spanish quickly, and the children were patient teachers as they tried to help us.

I spent much of my time helping with the farm animals—feeding the rabbits, pigs and chickens while picking up eggs from the laying hens to use in the home, and butchering the broilers and rabbits for meat in the home. A local village store would buy the hens we did not need and sell them live at their store, so I would regularly put several of them into a cage, load them on the steel-wheeled wheelbarrow, and go lumbering down the street to the village store about a mile away. We did not have a vehicle at the home. When we bought a new batch of chicks, I would bring them home on the public bus. When I bought groceries, I would sometimes bring them home in the wheelbarrow, but sometimes had them delivered. The United States government donated and delivered surplus supplies of rice, several kinds of beans, and cheese. Our "farmer" prepared the soil and planted banana and plantain plants, along with some other vegetables.

Eileen spent more time working with the children, but also working with the cooks to help prepare menus, and interpret recipes for them because they did not know how to read. The Department of Education would periodically send a teacher to help the children keep up on their studies. During the summer vacation, the enrollment at the home would reach its capacity of 50 children. During the school year, it often dropped to half that number.

By the middle of our two-year assignment, we were feeling comfortable with our work and the language, and Eileen was even helping teach a children's Sunday school class at the church. We could see ourselves serving long-term on the island, but also sensed that the Lord was leading us into a more direct leadership role in the church and its mission.

Then, a surprising letter arrived. My father wanted to know our specific plans after we finished our two-year assignment. If we were interested in the home farm, he would save it for us. If we were not interested, he was ready to sell it. That was a hard letter to answer. We took a week to pray and consider this option. The farm had belonged to my grandfather, and then to my father. We knew how fathers liked to have the home farm stay in the family. But, by the end of that week, we knew the farm was not for us. We knew God was calling us back to Latin America, but we would need to first get training for this responsibility. So, we painfully communicated that message to my father. What a relief it was when the next letter came. My older brother who had purchased with his wife his own farm fifty miles away several years earlier, found out that we were not interested in buying the home farm. They then decided to sell their farm and buy the home farm.

There was another challenge. I had not completed high school. I knew of a plan called General Educational Development (GED), designed primarily for veterans who had not completed high school and now wanted to attend college. I arranged for one of the local missionaries who was also an accredited teacher, to administer these tests, which I passed without difficulty. I was then accepted as a student at Eastern Mennonite College (now a university) in Harrisonburg, Virginia. Eileen would be able to complete her college at the same time. We were given permission to leave our assignment a couple weeks early so we could arrive on the campus in time for my freshman orientation. The Board of Directors of the children's home begged us to stay longer, but we knew God was leading us and opening doors for the next step in our pilgrimage.

It was a step of faith, as we had been serving for two years as volunteers, receiving room and board and each of us received $16 monthly for personal expenses. We had entered voluntary service after losing most of our possessions in a fire four months into our marriage. Surprisingly, we were able to accumulate enough funds for one semester of study. But, when God calls, He provides. It would be another step of faith.

Our experience in Puerto Rico was an excellent training ground for our future work. We were able to closely observe the church in another cultural setting, and visit the homes of the missionary families and hear their experiences. We were present at the ten-year celebration of the Puerto Rico Mennonite Conference when the first two Puerto Rican pastors were installed in the ministry.

One more unusual experience awaited us. We knew we were in an area which could be affected by hurricanes. Then, less than two weeks before our departure, it happened. The radio news warned everyone to prepare for storm warnings due to the effect of Hurricane Betsy. Then on the evening of August 11, the radio announcer said that storm warnings were changed to hurricane warnings. Then we lost our electricity and our access to the news on the radio.

We spent the next several hours getting food supplies on hand, nailing closed the shutters on the windows, and picking up loose items around the yard. By Sunday morning, August 12, the winds were strong with heavy rain, and none of us went to church. By 9:00 A.M. the wind was fierce. We knew part of the roof was gone because we could see daylight between the edge of the ceiling and the walls in a couple of the bedrooms. So, we moved all of the children into the basement dining room and waited it out. Water was running down the walls under the windows. Then suddenly, about 11:00 A.M., the wind stopped and the air was completely calm. We became aware that we were in the eye of Hurricane Betsy. After about an hour, the winds started up again with full force and water came in under the windows on the other side of the house. The winds gradually died down, and by about 4:00 P.M., we were able to go outside and survey the damage.

Many houses were missing roofs. Debris from broken trees lay everywhere. There was a long driveway into the children's home, and it was so full of fallen branches, that there was not even room to walk through. Our maintenance men cleaned it up so that vehicles could enter the driveway. The roof was gone from the hen house, and the rabbit houses were laying upside down and strewn around, with the rabbits fearfully hiding inside. We had no electricity, no running water, and no telephone. The home had a cistern to collect rainwater from the roof. The kitchen had a gas stove so we were able to boil the water to purify it, but there was no way to cool it. Boiled cistern water at room temperature tasted terrible, but at least, it was safe. We found our way around in the dark by candlelight. After a couple days, the U.S. Army provided fresh drinking water for us. It was still room temperature, but at least, it tasted much better.

When we left the island eleven days later on August 23, conditions were still in a mess. Many of the roads only had one-lane traffic due to landslides. But we said our good-byes and left, confident that the Lord would bring us back to Puerto Rico as long-term mission workers. We could not have imagined that the next time we would see Puerto Rico would be nine years later, and then only for a two-week visit. Our next visit was for one week 48 years later. How exciting it was to just follow the Lord a step at a time and see what surprises He had for us next!

Elmer reading to the children at Casa de Salud.

Elmer taking broilers to market by wheelbarrow.

Hauling people to church each Sunday.

Damage to driveway by Hurricane Betsy, August 12, 1956.

Our staff at Casa de Salud bidding us farewell.

Children at Casa de Salud saying good-bye.

Chapter 4

BACK TO THE BOOKS

Eileen

Our flight on August 23, 1956 from San Juan to La Guardia airport in New York City cost $64 each. My sister and her husband, who were living in eastern Pennsylvania at the time, met us there. They took us to northern New York to see our parents and siblings, and pack up and prepare for our college career. Elmer's father had stored our car, now five years old, and had started it up a couple times while we were gone just to warm up the engine.

Several days later, we packed our few belongings into the back of the car and headed south to Eastern Mennonite College in Harrisonburg, Virginia. This was before the days of interstate highways and the 535-mile trip would take anywhere from 12 ½ to 15 hours.

We moved into an 8 X 32 feet mobile home, which belonged to a local Christian believer and friend of the family. He rented it to us at a moderate price, and exercised abundant patience with us when we would get behind with our rental payments. The "trailer park" was owned by the college and was within easy walking distance of the campus. The dozen or so resident families were married students at the college. This "house trailer" became our home for the next five years, except for the first two summers when Elmer worked on what had been the home farm.

Elmer was now 25 years old, and except for several married students, most of his classmates were fresh out of high school. Elmer had been out of school for nine years. I enrolled part-time and was classified as a college junior. We could see ourselves working as a teaching couple, as I continued toward my degree in elementary education. Elmer enrolled in secondary education with a concentration in vocal music.

I picked up house-cleaning jobs on the side and Elmer picked up local jobs as they became available. Local farmers and others in the community would advertise at the college for jobs needing to be done. They could be as varied as helping harvest corn, picking apples, or cleaning out a chicken house. Payment was approximately $1 per hour.

In those days the faculty served for a sacrificial salary. Full-time tuition started at $202.50 per semester and increased $20 per semester each year, so that in our senior year, tuition was $262.50 per semester. We married students kept each other informed on where to find bargains, such as day-old bread at a local bakery, the best milk prices, local farm products, and where to buy gasoline. By the end of the first semester, our reserves were running dry, and we borrowed $500 from Elmer's father to get us through the first year.

Faculty members were deeply committed to the Lord and a good number of them served as pastors in local congregations. We were encouraged to plug into local congregations, and it was a refreshing experience each Sunday to leave the campus, going out into the real world as we drove to the country to a rural congregation. The first two years we attended two different churches, and the next three years we attended the same congregation in a place called Rawley Springs, the last village going west before climbing the mountain to cross into West Virginia. The Sunday school superintendent had pleaded with us to come and help them, and we were soon involved in worship leadership, Sunday school teaching, Vacation Bible School, and doing some home visitations.

Between Elmer's first and second year, as well as between his second and third year, we returned to New York State to work for Elmer's older brother on what had been the family farm. We moved into the upstairs apartment where we had lived just before going to Puerto Rico. We had a garden, which produced abundantly, and we canned a generous supply of garden produce to take back to Virginia with us, and even had a good supply of sweet corn to sell. God had richly provided.

A next-door neighbor could not understand why we made the decisions we did, and let Elmer know that if we would have stayed home the way we should have, we could now own the farm rather than Elmer merely being the hired man. Yes, the foolishness of God is wiser than the wisdom of man.

At the end of our first school year I was approached by a board member of a local Christian school and was offered a job teaching the first four grades. The school was located on a riverbank so it was called Bank Mennonite School. The salary was modest, $1800 per year, but it provided full-time employment. We were even able to pay back Elmer's father for the money we had borrowed. I continued to take classes late in the day, and Elmer continued full-time and picked up jobs on Saturday. I taught for two years and the next summer we stayed in Virginia so I could take summer school while Elmer worked for a local carpenter.

During our senior year an opportunity came for me to be a kindergarten teacher. At the church we had attended during our second college year, there were now several children who were a few weeks too young to enter the regular school system. The parents got together and invited me to set up a kindergarten class in the basement of one of the parent couple's house. I had twelve students and was able to arrange my schedule so I could teach three afternoons a week and take the courses I needed to receive my degree.

During Elmer's sophomore year he kept being nudged by the Holy Spirit, telling him, "I want you in the ministry." Finally, Elmer was convinced, went to the dean's office and asked to change his major from secondary education to Bible and the Pastoral Ministries Program. The first two years were not wasted by any means, but it did mean a change in curriculum. So, as he began his third year, he concentrated for hours over New Testament Greek vocabulary, along with other courses in the pastoral ministries program.

Then an opportunity came for Elmer. A local believer had a contract with the United States Postal Service to deliver mail on what was called Star Route. This Christian brother was looking for someone to drive part-time, as it was an 11-hour day, six days a week schedule. He had a van and would haul bulk mail to eight post offices out through the country into West Virginia, and service 175 rural delivery mailboxes. It was a 125-mile trip each day.

Elmer gladly took this job for the next two years as a Saturday job, as well as on other days when there were breaks in the school schedule. He worked up to four days a week during the summer months. Again, pay was $1 per hour, but it was steady work. At a couple of the places, there was a short layover to wait for incoming mail and Elmer could eat his packed lunch and study while getting paid.

As we approached graduation in 1960, two significant events occurred. One, the emerging seminary was developing into a three-year program. The academic dean of the seminary talked with those of us who were Bible majors, and encouraged us to return for seminary. He was very convincing. Secondly, we received a visit from Mark Peachey, who was the missions director for Conservative Mennonite Conference. We had contemplated returning to Latin America under the Mennonite Board of Missions.

The Mennonite Church is composed of a number of area conferences that also carry on overseas ministries. Our home congregation in New York State is affiliated with the Conservative Mennonite Conference. Mark Peachey knew about our interest in Latin America, and he came to the campus and asked to talk with us. The mission board of our area conference was planning to open work somewhere in Central America and he wanted us to know that they were interested in our availability.

Our college graduation came in June 1960. We were two of the 90 graduates. Interestingly, fourteen of the graduates were married. There were also five engaged couples among the graduates. I received a Bachelor of Arts in Elementary Education, and Elmer received a Bachelor of Arts with a concentration in Bible and Pastoral Ministries. He had gone straight through in four years, with my faithful support as the primary breadwinner. I had started college in 1949, and after years of part-time studies, we graduated together.

Now we needed to respond to the request from Mark Peachey. After two years in Puerto Rico, and four years at Eastern Mennonite College, we felt out of touch with the Conservative Mennonite Conference. The annual Conference sessions were held that summer in August in Kalona, Iowa. We decided to attend as we sought God's direction for our next step. We returned to New York State to see family members and there we joined my parents and my older brother, who was serving on the mission board at the time and had given them our name. We stopped twice overnight as we covered the 1,000 miles in pre-interstate highway days.

When Mark Peachey and the mission board members found out that we were on the conference grounds, they asked to meet with us. They informed us that after an investigative trip, Costa Rica had been chosen. Then they wanted us to know this: the Mission Board had already accepted us. Would we now accept them? The next day was the final day of our Conference sessions. They wanted our answer before the sessions ended.

What a night that was! We were staying in a farmhouse of one of the local believers, and that upstairs bedroom remains entrenched in our memory. We prayed and we struggled. Yes, we felt called to Latin America, but now we were being asked to go to a new field and start from nothing. We felt so inadequate. We cannot say that we have ever heard the Lord speak to us in an audible voice. Yet, His voice seemed so clear as His words were impressed upon us. "You have been preparing for this all these years. If you say no, what is your reason?"

We continued to hesitate. Those words came to us again and again. Finally, we said yes. But, Elmer was committed to a year of study at the seminary.

The next day we met with the mission board. We informed them that we were ready to commit to this assignment, but we would not be ready until Elmer finished a year of seminary. They looked at each other and one of them answered for the group, "We'll wait." We left the grounds as missionaries under appointment.

It was back to the college campus, as Elmer became one of thirteen seminary students. Among those thirteen, we even organized a men's octet, and not surprisingly, Elmer was one of its members. I, as a college graduate, received employment as an instructor in a Weekday Religious Education program where students with the written permission of their parents, were given released time to receive Bible classes. They were in the public schools, but the program was funded by local churches, with ninety percent of the students participating. I loved the opportunity to dig into the Word of God as I taught these classes.

In our senior year we had again borrowed $500 from Elmer's father, interest-free, as we were both studying. Seminary tuition was only $110 per semester, and Elmer was given a $100 scholarship for each semester. Through my employment, we were able to repay $200. Then my brother-in-law donated $200 toward our debt. We were at rest because we felt our ten-year old vehicle would be worth $100, giving us enough to pay off our debt.

As the year of seminary drew to a close, plans were made for an ordination. On July 2, 1961 we sat in the home of the

presiding bishop who would be in charge of the ordination service. Mark Peachey as the Missions Director met with us and
would be preaching the sermon. We had filled out no question-
naires and only had brief interviews with those in charge. As
our interview came to a close, Mark asked if we had any further
questions. Elmer had one more. How did they know us well
enough to give us this responsibility? Mark chuckled and said,
"We did our homework. We have received a good report."

That evening the Croghan Mennonite Church building
was packed full. It held several hundred people, but every seat
was taken. As we sat in the front row, even before the service began, we heard the ushers placing folding chairs into the
aisles to accommodate the large crowd. What an affirmation
for our ministry!

After Mark's sermon, taken from II Timothy 4, the local
bishop representing the local church, my father representing
the family, and the chairman of the mission board representing the mission agency all placed their hands upon Elmer
as the two of us knelt side-by-side to receive the ordination
charge. The words came to us so powerfully from Psalm
119:57, "You are my portion, O Lord; I have promised to
obey your words."

Two days later, we left on an extended trip of 4,000 miles,
going as far south as Arkansas and as far west as Kansas, visiting
congregations that were part of our constituency. Some people
questioned the wisdom of starting on a trip like this in a well-
worn vehicle, but that was what we had. True, we had to add oil
almost every time we filled the gas tank, but other than that, the
only problem we faced was a flat tire in El Dorado, Arkansas,
where we had spent the night with a small congregation. After

getting that fixed the next morning, we were on our way. Our trip took us to hot Kansas in mid-July with no air conditioning, but we survived the inconvenience.

At a congregation in northeast Indiana, the pastor announced that they wanted to take a love offering for us that evening. He suggested that we, perhaps, still had college debts. We had told no one of the $100 that we still owed. The love offering that evening in that relatively small congregation came to $100.38. We could pay off our debt!

Several days later, on the day before we left for Costa Rica, we sold the vehicle for $100. In those days, a ten-year-old vehicle with 100,000 miles was considered about worn out. We were able to take that money with us to get started in Costa Rica. The vehicle had served us well, and we were debt-free. We had lived on a tight budget for the past five years with quite a variety of jobs, but we were never hungry. We did not always have all we wanted, but we always had all we needed. God provided, one step at a time.

Eileen's students at Bank Mennonite School, grades 1 – 4.

Eileen's kindergarten class during senior year of college.

Elmer delivering mail at his Saturday job.

Receiving our college degrees from Eastern Mennonite College,
June 1960.

Chapter 5

WELCOME TO "TICOLANDIA"

Elmer

It had been exactly five years to the day since our last plane ride from San Juan, Puerto Rico to La Guardia Airport in New York City. It was now August 23, 1961, and we were on a plane headed to San José, Costa Rica. This small Central American country was sandwiched between Nicaragua and Panama. Bordering both the Atlantic and Pacific Oceans, geographically, it is the size of West Virginia and seemed almost as mountainous with volcanic peaks as high as 13,000 feet above sea level. The population in 1961 was 1,300,000. It was known as Tico Land because the Costa Rican people tended to use the expression "tico" at the end of descriptive words. For example, "chiquito" is small; "chiquitico" is very small.

We were traveling with Raymond and Susan Schlabach and their infant daughter from Plain City, Ohio. Our mission agency had appointed them to work in Bible translation among the Bribri Indigenous people in Talamanca in southeastern Costa Rica. We would serve as a support couple for them while establishing a Spanish-speaking church in one of the urban areas.

Our first task, after getting settled, was to study the language. The Spanish Language Institute is located in San José as a center to prepare missionaries linguistically and culturally to serve in Spanish-speaking countries throughout the world. More than 130 mission agencies used this facility. There were three fifteen-week terms each year, with a break of a couple of weeks between each term. Ideally, missionaries who had no background in the language would stay for a year, although many stayed for two terms, instead of three. A fifteen-week refresher course was offered to persons with a background in Spanish. We found ourselves in classes with missionaries who had spent up to five years in the field and were now taking this refresher course before returning to their assignment. We had spent two years in the field and five years back in the States, so it was a challenge. Thankfully, we caught on quickly.

The Language Institute had established a Big Brother-Little Brother program, whereby present students would sign up to meet incoming students, help them get established by arranging housing for them, show them the bus routes, and help them to find their way around the city. We were blessed to have as a Big Brother couple, James and Rhoda Sauder.

Eileen and I had known them for five years as he and I had gone through college together. The Sauder family was now under assignment to Honduras under a sister Mennonite agency in Pennsylvania. They had found an upstairs two-bedroom furnished apartment for us, which was located a 20-minute bus ride from the Language Institute. We boarded the public bus with our luggage, piled in the back, and made our way from the airport to the bus station in San José. We then piled our luggage on the roof of a taxi and made our way to our apartment, which would become home to us for seven months. This gave us time for a term of language study, followed by three months "to spy out" the land.

Five days after our arrival, we sat in classes, which were usually limited to four or five persons in each class, all taught by persons who spoke Spanish as their primary language. Approximately thirty instructors were to teach subjects as varied as grammar, phonetics, and public speaking. Basic equipment included a tape recorder where students recorded their work and had it evaluated. This was before the days of cassette players and much less, all the gadgets and modern equipment presently available that we ourselves don't even understand.

There was a chapel service each day and a spiritual emphasis week each term. Special lectures were given for greater cultural understanding. To effectively communicate, much more than language proficiency was needed. The leadership of the Institute diligently worked at helping us understand the culture. Outings were arranged many Saturdays to see interesting sights where we usually travelled in three chartered busses. We were encouraged to visit local churches on Sunday, and a lengthy list of churches with their addresses was given. There was a Language School choir and we were invited to sing in a number of local churches.

While in language school, we investigated possible locations to begin our ministry. Our mission agency had assigned us to Costa Rica but did not tell us in what city, except to be available to assist the other missionary couple, the Schlabach family, where needed. We knew we were unable to reach 1,300,000 people. We needed to decide where to locate.

We made contact with several other mission agencies working in the country. A key contact came as we met with a local Christian businessman who was president of what was known as the Costa Rican Evangelical Alliance. This organization had no authority over the churches, but existed to facilitate the work of the churches and keep information flowing so that the various agencies could work in a harmonious way. The Board of Directors was composed of nine members, with no more than two members from the same entity.

The president of the Board was most interested in hearing about our plans and made it clear to us that if we were there to work in harmony with the groups already in the country, there was plenty of room for us. If we were there to compete with other groups, there was no room for us. We informed him that we recognized that God was at work through many agencies, but we also recognized that the Great Commission was for our churches as well. We had every intention to cooperate with what God was doing through other agencies and churches. At that time, only three and a half percent of the total population was considered as evangelical Christian. The vast majority of the people considered themselves as Roman Catholic, but sadly, a large percentage of them had no personal relationship with the Lord, nor knew what it meant to follow Jesus in a life of discipleship.

In conversing with another seasoned missionary in the country we mentioned the possibility of settling in Limón, the Atlantic seaport city close to where the Schlabach family would be located. The missionary advised us that since so much legal activity needed to be taken care of in the capital city, we should have a center close to San José. Many of the agencies already had churches in the major San José area, but the city of Heredia, located only eight miles from San José, and between the airport and the capital city, had 17,500 people and only one small evangelical church, affiliated with the Southern Baptist Convention, consisting of about sixty people. Heredia was close enough to San José, and conveniently located for us to attend to legal matters, and at 3,800 feet altitude, it would give the Schlabach family a pleasant change of climate on the occasions when they wanted to get away from the Talamanca tropics.

Following language study in early December, Raymond and I travelled to Talamanca to check out the future location of the work of the Schlabach family. The trip involved starting out on a 5:00 A.M. bus for the airport, boarding a plane at 7:00 A.M. for a 40-minute flight to Limón on the seacoast, riding a train for one hour and 45 minutes to a village called Penshurst, crossing the river in a dugout canoe, and then boarding an open-sided mule car for a one hour and 20-minute ride to Cahuita. The mule car seated fifteen to twenty people on backless benches, and yes, a mule on a narrow-gauge track pulled the car. In Cahuita there was a rustic road and transportation was provided in an old bus, and at the end of the line, Raymond and I found private transportation into Bambú, which would eventually become the home for him and his wife and daughters.

Coming back to plans for our future, I visited Heredia and the pastor, Oscar Gómez, from the local Baptist Church, to let him know of our intentions. We desired to start a second evangelical church in this city of 17,500 people, while showing proper respect to their congregation for the work they were doing. Pastor Gomez was kind and courteous, although cautious, and we knew we would need to proceed carefully to earn his respect. He informed me that finding a house to rent would be a difficult task, as people in Heredia did not like to rent to evangelical believers. He told us of a house across town; ten blocks away from their church facilities, where one of their members lived that planned to move to the next city, which had a somewhat lower altitude and warmer climate. Pastor Gómez had no idea who owned the house.

I went to the house and talked with the lady, who with her husband, was planning to move out. She told me a lawyer in the capital city of San José owned the house. He was an open-minded man and she was sure he would rent the house to us if we did not tell him why we wanted it.

I checked in the phone directory and located the office of the lawyer. I prayed intensely about this and felt this would be the sign the Lord would give us. If the lawyer would rent the house to us, this is where we should locate. If he would not rent us the house, this meant we should look elsewhere. I fearfully made my way to the lawyer's office, while inwardly hoping the lawyer would not rent the house to us, freeing us to go elsewhere. We had heard that Heredia was a difficult town to work in, and over the last several decades, five groups tried it and gave up, until the Baptists succeeded seven years before our arrival.

The lawyer was busy so I waited for my turn. The Lawyer called me in and asked, "How may I help you?" I timidly responded, "I would like to rent your house that you own in Heredia." The lawyer looked at me rather sternly through thick glasses and asked, "Are you a Protestant?" I replied, "Yes, I am. Does that make a difference?" The lawyer responded, "No, it does not make a difference to me. But, if you are choosing Heredia, you are choosing a hard place. But, I will rent the house to you."

We did not need to tell him why we wanted it. Then he proceeded to advise me not to go from door to door like the Jehovah's Witnesses and the Mormons do, as that just turns people off. He told me the people in Heredia were fanatically Roman Catholic and think all non-Catholics are atheists. He also advised us to move in and make friends and build relationships. Here he was, a Catholic lawyer, telling us what strategy to use to win over the Catholics.

The owner wanted us to sign a minimal one-year contract. We were not convinced we would last one year and asked for a six-month contract and the owner consented. They were doing some repair work on the house and it was not ready for a few weeks. In fact, the owner begged me to keep Eileen from seeing the house until they were able to mend some of the rat holes in the wall. We went around buying furniture, and the moving day finally came on March 26, 1962. We became residents of the city of Heredia, and lived in that house for more than

21 years. It also became the location of the first Mennonite Church in Costa Rica.

We knew no one in Heredia except the Baptist pastor and his family. How would we begin? The lawyer landlord's advice was to gradually make friends and build relationships. We call that friendship evangelism. We agreed that it was wise advice.

Arrival in Costa Rica and taxi to our apartment, August 23, 1961.

Heredia Mennonite Church in 1964 as part of our residence.

Chapter 6

GOING FORWARD

Eileen

"For this God is our God for ever and ever; he will be our guide even to the end." Psalm 48:14. A friend once told us that God always leads him into places where he feels the most afraid. We were aware that we were now in a city of opportunity, but we were warned that Heredia would be difficult. We should expect opposition. How and where should we begin? The first opportunity soon came.

We had just moved in and we needed to buy a few groceries for supper. Our next-door neighbor saw us and came over to get acquainted. We asked her where we could buy some milk and bread. She referred us to a bakery two blocks from the house, which was open until late in the evening. Elmer walked up there and the clerk, Marta waited on him. She recognized him as a North American and wondered what he was doing in Heredia. He told her we were there to start an evangelical church. She asked him if he visited homes. "Yes, we do." Of course, we had not yet done so, as we had just arrived. Then she asked, "Would you visit my home?" God had provided our first contact.

I visited that home regularly, and although Marta became a long-lasting friend, she never committed her life to Christ. Then one day, Marta's fellow worker, Irene complained to me that I kept visiting Marta but never visited her. So, I started visiting Irene. But, she also never committed her life to Christ. On one of my visits, Irene had a visit from her sister-in-law, Isabel. I found this young mother to be spiritually hungry, and Isabel became a new believer in Christ and an active participant in our emerging congregation.

God had led us to a house on a busy street corner only two blocks from the city's central market. Our front door opened directly to the sidewalk along the front of the house, which was right next to the street. It did not seem wise to try to pass out literature to the public, but we often kept the front door open with a rack full of Christian literature visible and available for the taking. Although a small amount of tracts would be taken and torn up in front of the house, a vast majority was taken to read, and a good number of people returned again and again for more literature. At times, someone would even knock when the door was closed and ask for literature. We also placed a display in one of our windows with a large print open Bible on an attractive background and a lighted lamp beside it. It seemed that several persons would stop each day and read the passage, which was displayed. How much fruit came from all of these efforts? We have no way of knowing, but we knew that the only way to get an abundant harvest was to sow abundantly.

Our first Sunday morning service was held two days after moving in, and it was small—very small. We now had a six-month-old daughter (more about that later) and had hired a 16-year-old girl to work for us and help out in child care and house work. She decided to stay for that first service. There was Elmer, our baby, our hired hand, and myself—the four of us in all—that is how we started.

Another contact was with the Carvajal family. A couple from Colombia (Armando and Eunice Hernandez) were studying at the Latin America Biblical Seminary in San Jose and giving pastoral leadership to a small congregation in San José. Two young brothers were preparing for baptism in that congregation when the family suddenly moved to Heredia. Armando and Eunice visited us one Sunday for our morning service, and expressed how they wished they knew where the Carvajal family lived so that we could make contact with them. Just then, Eunice glanced out the window and saw Orlando Carvajal going by the house. She quickly called to him and discovered that the family lived less than two blocks from our house. We quickly made contact, and within several weeks the two Carvaial brothers were baptized in our church, and Orlando eventually became our first Costa Rican pastor. He has provided pastoral leadership in several outlying congregations, and although now at retirement age, he continues in active leadership.

A third contact came by means of a radio broadcast Luz y Verdad (Light and Truth). The broadcast, originating in Puerto Rico, could be heard each week on our local evangelical radio station. A friend of ours, Lester Hershey, was a missionary pastor in Puerto Rico and we knew him and his family when we were there. Lester was coming to Costa Rica for some meetings having to do with Christian radio, and we invited him to have special meetings at our church. We announced those meetings on the radio, and Jovita Corrales heard the announcement. Until then she had not known that there was an evangelical church in Heredia. Although unable to come to those meetings, she wrote down the address and later visited us on a Sunday evening.

I then visited her home and she gave her life to Christ. Her husband Eladio hesitated, but after nine months of observing his wife's life, and then several conversations between he and Elmer, Eladio also gave his life to Christ. Eladio and Jovita were later able to meet our friend Lester Hershey. Eladio and Lester were very close in age and became dear friends. Lester Hershey, as a seasoned missionary, became a mentor to us as he shared from his vast experience. It is always wise to hear from those who have preceded us, and we always enjoyed Lester's periodic visits.

These were examples of what was happening. We diligently followed every lead, and walked many miles all over town. Scripture speaks of four kinds of soil and we know that is true. Some persons showed interest but that was as far as it went. Some made decisions for Christ but it was like the rocky soil or like the soil with thorns, and they dropped out. But, some of the seed fell on good soil and produced a harvest. Many of our continued contacts came through those people who were now in the church, as friends reached out to friends, relatives reached out to relatives, and neighbors reached out to neighbors. Lester Hershey had told us that our church would grow through our sweat and tears. He had been there. Mark Peachey, our Missions Director in our home office, liked to remind us that we needed to practice both "flexibility and stickability." He was right.

When we began having services, we opened a corner door from our living room to the street to welcome people. But, it held our living room furniture. Another friend attended several times but did not continue; yet he gave us some good advice. He suggested that we should have church benches, because people do not like to enter private homes unless they are personally invited. So, we moved our living room into a smaller room. We went to a small cabinet shop just several feet up the street and had the gentleman there make several church benches so that we could accommodate about thirty people. We also put a church sign over the door. People responded, and we crowded up to 52 people into that former living room, now a small chapel. The work developed slowly, but there was progress.

In October 1962, we had our first baptism. In August 1963, we baptized the two Carvajal brothers. In May 1964, we baptized a fourth person. We had been in Heredia more than two years and had four members. Was it worth all the sweat, prayer, and tears? Then in 1965 we saw an encouraging change. It took flexibility and stickability, but eight more members were received, and we now had twelve members. The first four were young people, but now we had families. We held our first congregational meeting on July 14, 1965, and organized our first congregation, the Heredia Mennonite Church.

Sadly, alcoholism was a major social problem in Heredia, and on several occasions persons under the influence of alcohol would come in during worship services. Some were respectful. Others were disruptive, and we had to deal with them kindly but firmly. Another common practice was for men to have a lover in addition to their wife. A number of men who came into the church had fathered children out of wedlock. As they came to Christ, life was radically changed. Another issue was others who were attracted by Spiritualism and consulted with mediums to make contact with the dead. The closest medium lived next door to us, but years later her daughter and husband gave their lives to Christ.

As neighbors discovered who we were, some complained to our landlord for letting us rent that house. He later told us that someone had been interested in renting the house to use as a nightclub with late-night activity and questionable sexual activity. He asked these neighbors who they wanted to be there—our family or a nightclub. They readily admitted that we were "good people" and he should let us stay there. Over the years, we developed cordial relationships with these neighbors.

What was daily activity like? Once when my mother visited us, she remarked that the telephone and the doorbell determined our day's activity. True, we did much visitation as we followed up on leads that came in various ways, and I spent many hours in Bible study with the ladies who came, but the phone and the doorbell frequently called for our attention.

We had a guest room with its own bathroom, and we entertained hundreds of guests who travelled through from North America, as well as youth and families who would visit the city from rural isolated villages where our churches were also at work.

As the congregation grew, we removed one wall from the former living room, and then another wall. Sunday school classes were held in different rooms throughout the house. It then became evident that the congregation would need a larger facility. After looking at dozens of possibilities, we decided on one that was seven blocks to the north, on another very visible street corner.

However, we ran into another problem. The word got around that we were looking for a property for a church building, and people warned the owner not to sell to us evangelical Christians, even though she was personally ready to do so. We finally reached an agreement with her. We had a program of Voluntary Service for short-term youth workers, and the director was an agronomist. She would sell the property to this North American agronomist, and that would protect her. What he did with the property would be up to him, and it would be none of her business. After several months, he then transferred the property to our church. True, we had to pay for closing costs two times, but we obtained the property that we wanted.

We again tore out walls in the large house on the property, and at the first service at the new location on February 16, 1969, our attendance was 116. In the house we lived in that we used as our former church facility, we could now utilize the rooms as intended. Although there was only a small outdoor patio, we now had a twelve-room house to comfortably accommodate our family and to receive guests.

We now took up the challenge of paying a building loan. A number of women were skilled in embroidery and volunteered their time to do souvenirs. I designed the souvenirs and provided the materials to the ladies to do typical aprons, placemats, tea towels, and potholders. With many visitors coming through, there was a ready market for these souvenirs. The funds raised helped significantly to pay off the loan.

Drama was an effective part of our ministry. Special seasons of the year, like Christmas and Easter were excellent times to present drama with an effective Christian message. I usually directed these, and Elmer often was a character in the drama, along with a sizeable group of young people. Besides preparing these for the Heredia congregation, we were invited to present them in several surrounding congregations and villages.

Villages of 2,000 to 3,000 people surrounded the city of Heredia, and we followed up on contacts that had been made in these villages. Often we started in a home, where I would teach the children in one room with flannelgraph Bible stories, and Elmer would have a Bible study with adults in the next room. We had the joy of seeing satellite congregations emerge in five of these communities, each with Costa Rican leadership.

What was our approach in church planting? What was our strategy? Some say *this* is the way you should do it, or *that* is the way you should do it. We merely followed the doors God had opened. We sowed abundantly and sought to disciple those who responded. God gave the increase.

Dedication of the new Heredia church building, February 16, 1969.

Congregation following dedication service.

Early church leaders in Heredia.

Installing a Costa Rican pastor.

Chapter 7

GROWING A FAMILY

Elmer

Eight years had passed since our wedding day. By now we expected to have a family. We even had medical checkups and were told that it may not be as easy for us to have children, but it should be possible. However, it did not happen, so we looked into adoption.

We began the process while studying in Virginia and had the possibility of adopting a child there. But, time was limited and it would have been impossible to finish the adoption procedure before the time to leave for Costa Rica. We made contact with the director of the Spanish Language Institute in Costa Rica, and he encouraged us to wait until we arrived in Costa Rica. Adoptions were relatively easy there.

We entered language study and within several weeks we received this information: a Presbyterian medical doctor and his wife were in the Language Institute preparing to go to Ecuador. They had no children, so he put a notice in the local newspaper, expressing their interest in adoption and exploring possibilities.

They made it clear that the adoption would need to go through the proper legal channels.

They were surprised to receive eight responses. Some were from people who wanted to help them out and hopefully get paid for it. They studied each response and concluded that there were three cases worthy of considering. They decided on a child yet to be born. A couple assigned to Mexico accepted the case of another child yet to be born. Both turned out to be boys. We were invited to receive the third case, that of a 3 ½ month old girl. She was born on August 1, 1961, three weeks before we arrived in Costa Rica.

On November 15, 1961 at 2:00 P.M., we sat in the office of a Christian medical doctor and waited for the doctor to call us in to see the child, who would be brought in by her mother. She was a single mother with a low-paying job and wanted the child to have a good home with parents who could provide for her. The doctor checked the child over and assured us that with tender loving care, and good nutrition, the child would develop well. At 4:30 that afternoon we sat in a lawyer's office and were handed the 3½ month old baby weighing seven pounds, whom we named Emily Rosa. With good nutrition, she gained almost one pound per week for several weeks and walked well before her first birthday.

The three children mentioned above, all found homes among students at the Spanish Language Institute, preparing for a missionary career. They ended up in three different countries—Ecuador, Mexico, and Costa Rica.

The legal process can be time-consuming and a somewhat anxious time, as a child is first given temporary placement, followed by a thirty-day waiting period. Then the child is given permanent placement, followed by another thirty-day waiting period. Then the child is declared eligible for adoption, followed by another thirty-day waiting period. If anyone is opposed in any way during any step in this procedure, especially anyone in the birth family, they have the right to protest. It was always a relief to get through these three procedures without opposition. Naturalization as a United States citizen was still pending until a return visit to the United States.

As Emily approached two years of age, we decided we wanted to receive another child. We put our own announcement in the newspaper and received one favorable response. A young lady from a distant community had come into the capital city to work, and found employment doing housework for a well-to-do couple. While there, she discovered she was pregnant and did not want her parents to know. She wanted to place the child with an adoptive family as soon as the child was born, so she could again return home to visit her parents, and not let them know what had happened.

Her employer served as the contact with us, and we arranged to have the child born in the evangelical hospital at our expense. We would take the child, whether a boy or a girl. At that time we had no phone, so we kept in contact with our medical doctor every few days. One day when Elmer had access to a phone, he called the doctor and was informed that we were parents of a new daughter, born the previous day on July 21, 1963, weighing six pounds, nine ounces. On July 23, we brought our two-day-old daughter, Elnora Jane, home from the hospital.

Our first term in Costa Rica began in 1961, and in 1964 we made our first trip back to our home community in the

United States. We were delighted to introduce our parents to their two new grandchildren.

After a couple years we decided it was time to explore having a son. We became aware that we could go through the Costa Rican social services department for a child. They had a children's home that was vastly overcrowded. It took several weeks to get all the papers in order to be approved by this agency. Then, one day we were handed a paper of authorization to take to the children's home and see four boys, all available for adoption. We could have any or all of the four. We felt one boy was enough at the time, and realized what a difference our decision would make for one of those four boys. We chose the one who seemed most alert and responsive to us. There were a few more details to finalize, and on the next day, April 8, 1967, we took our son, Erland Ray home with us. He was born on October 27, 1965. Although he was a year and a half old, he had basically spent his time as one of three boys in one crib, and could not walk nor even stand. His two older sisters were excellent teachers, and within a few weeks he was walking.

On a later visit to the social services agency, the personnel were amazed to see our son's development and called in several co-workers to see him. They let us know that they were ready to place more children with us as soon as we wanted them. It would have been hard to imagine when Erland came to us not using his legs, that by the time he was a senior in high school, he would be voted as the most valuable player on the high school soccer team, having made more goals than any other player. On our next trip to the United States in 1967 we had three children to display.

By the time Erland reached his second birthday, we decided we would like for him to have a brother. We checked with the social services agency and they gave us this news. They did not have *a* son for us. They only had two sons, as twin brothers were in urgent need of a good home. At six months of age, they weighed nine pounds and ten and a half pounds respectively.

When we hesitated to take on this responsibility, they praised Eileen on what a good mother she was and they knew she could do it. We went home and got ready for two babies, and the next day, November 8, 1968, we brought two boys home with us, born April 30, 1968. Our first three children, and us, their parents, all had names starting with the letter E. It seemed that seven E's in the family was going to be too many. Since our fathers both had names starting with E, we decided to use those as middle names, so we named them Marvin Elmer and Melvin Elias.

The twin boys needed extra medical attention for several weeks, and thankfully, a medical doctor was located less than three blocks from our house. He was willing to come to our house and give them the attention they needed whenever we called him. They responded well to the doctor's several visits and to the medications he prescribed. They developed into healthy little boys. On our next visit to the United States we were seven. We had our daughters naturalized as United States citizens in 1964 and our three sons were naturalized on our third visit in 1970.

Our children were a huge blessing as we related to families in the Heredia community. It seemed wise to place them in the public school system, where elementary schools were divided between boys' schools and girls' schools. All children dressed alike with matching uniforms. It made it easy for the children to know what to wear each day.

The public school system was of excellent quality academically, but we discovered that it was frustrating for our children to only have a speaking knowledge of the English language and not be able to read or write in English. They would receive letters from their cousins but not be able to answer them. Although our children all started in local public schools, we gradually transferred them to English-speaking schools so they could be thoroughly bi-lingual.

As of this writing in 2018, four of our five children are married; we have nine grandchildren of whom four are married, and we have four great-grandchildren. Our family is scattered into eight different communities. We deeply enjoy our God-given family.

Elmer, Eileen, and the three older children in 1968.

Twins Marvin and Melvin on first birthday, April 30, 1969.

Our three older children in school uniforms, Emily and Elnora for elementary school, and Erland for kindergarten, 1971.

Our five children as a happy family in 1975.

Chapter 8

EXTENDING OUR BORDERS

Eileen

Our focus, so far, had been on the city of Heredia, a provincial capital located eight miles from the capital city of San José. But, we were not alone as a missionary family in Costa Rica. Our mission agency, Rosedale Mennonite Missions, had as many as four long-term missionary families serving in Costa Rica at various locations in direct church leadership. The team also included as many as 12 to15 short-term volunteers who usually gave thirty months of service to Costa Rica. They were primarily involved in a variety of social services in the name of Christ, and worked closely with the churches that were located in their communities of service. They worked in medical clinics, literacy, agricultural development, community service, and in assisting long-term personnel. Although their work was directed more toward meeting physical needs, one of our Costa Rican friends referred to them as "Walking Sermons."

As an association of churches in North America, known as Conservative Mennonite Conference, we did not focus upon establishing mega-churches, but rather, on establishing relatively small fellowship churches, and in clusters where they could relate to each other. In our North American conference of just over 100 congregations, sixty percent of them had fewer than 100 active members. Another twenty-seven percent had between 100 and 200 members. Only thirteen percent had more than 200 members, with the largest having just over 700 members. The average size was 115 members. Only a small handful of our church buildings could seat more than 1,000 people.

We carried that same concept into our program in Costa Rica. Presently only two congregations have more than 100 members, and the average size is about 60 members. The country of Costa Rica is divided into seven provinces and we have established congregations in four of them, and in four area clusters. The largest group is in the San José-Heredia urban area with eight congregations, and smaller congregational clusters in three rural areas—southeastern Costa Rica in Talamanca near the Panama border, northern Costa Rica in the Sarapiquí region, and northwestern Costa Rica in the Upala area near the Nicaragua border.

As congregations developed in the different areas, Elmer decided in late 1972 to call for a meeting of the various leaders, both missionaries and Costa Ricans. We wanted to discern a good way to relate to each other from our various locations. A recommendation arose out of that meeting to organize a Costa Rican Conference of Mennonite Churches, and a committee was named of two missionaries and four Costa Ricans to prepare a constitution and do the groundwork to legally organize an association of churches. Elmer was asked to preside this committee and diligent work was done, and many hours were invested over the next months. On the last weekend of March 1974, the first annual meeting was held and resulted in the official organization of the Conference of Mennonite Churches of Costa Rica. Elmer was named as its first president and served for six years until a Costa Rican brother was chosen to replace him.

Elmer continued to fulfill roles in both our mission agency and in the Costa Rican Mennonite Conference. Some of his roles included being a church planter, serving as pastor, and serving as the legal representative for our mission agency which included signing official documents for residence permits for North American personnel, and processing the purchase of church properties and mission vehicles. He also served as the Missions Treasurer on the field. In the national conference he served in administrative roles, as an overseer or mentor, and in leadership preparation. He made frequent trips to our churches in the outlying communities, often over rough roads or by bouncing along by plane, until an improved highway system was developed.

It was not always smooth sailing. The enemy tried to disrupt where he could. On one occasion Elmer needed to be directly involved when a group of men, mostly from one extended family, became divisive and critical of the church for allowing women to speak during church service, for using teaching materials other than the Bible, for teaching the tithe, and for giving instruction for baptism. Sadly, it resulted in these men and their families leaving the congregation. We tried to help them organize as a separate congregation affiliated with the Conference, but that only lasted for a short time until they decided to become independent. Even then, we were able to continue a positive relationship with them.

There were a couple other cases where pastors fell into immorality and had to be removed from their pastorate. Those were painful times as Elmer worked closely with the local church leaders in confronting these issues. God does not promise an easy road, but He promises to be with us.

There were two overwhelming experiences when we lost a fellow worker. One was a 20-year-old young man who drowned. The other was a 28-year-old medical worker who died of septicemia, a blood disease, after a short illness. We needed to give leadership in each case to inform the family and to make funeral arrangements. We had not gone to Costa Rica to choose caskets for fellow workers. We were not taught in any of our college or graduate courses how to do this. We had to do it in October 1968 and again in April 1970.

Yet, the church marched on. For several years there were three evangelical churches in the city of Heredia, each quite different from one another. One was a typical Baptist Church; another was a typical Pentecostal Church, along with our Mennonite Church. It was delightful for the three pastors to sit down each week and share and pray together and to regularly exchange pulpits.

As I became less involved in the local congregation, I committed to become a special education instructor at a bi-lingual school, and thus help cover the cost of our children's tuition. I became actively involved in the mothers' meetings of our school-age children, and my testimony soon became well known. I was an active participant and counselor in a chapter of Women's Aglow, an international women's ministry. I was Director of Christian Education of the Costa Rica Mennonite Conference for several years and did teacher training in all of our church communities.

Elmer gradually became involved in a variety of interdenominational activities. Alfalit was a literacy and literature program based in Costa Rica, serving all of Latin America. The Costa Rica Evangelical Alliance was made up of a majority of the evangelical mission and church groups working in Costa Rica, and was a good way to keep in touch with each other and cooperate in the extension of the Kingdom of God. We can experience unity in Christ without all needing to belong to the same organization.

Good Will Caravans was a ministry to meet social and medical needs of rural communities, sending a team of several persons from various denominations to a rural community for one week at a time, and thus, reaching a number of communities. Along with meeting social needs, films were shown each evening with an evangelistic emphasis. The Spanish Language Institute served missionaries from many agencies that had been assigned to many countries throughout the Spanish-speaking world. There was the Roble Alto children's ministry, which operated a children's home and some day care centers. Elmer served on all of these committees at some time during these years. The Heredia Mennonite congregation was also active in the children's home especially at Christmastime, with visits from our women's group who made toys and dolls and other handmade gifts and gave special programs.

In addition to these ongoing ministries, there were a number of interdenominational pastors' retreats and nationwide evangelistic crusades. Elmer served on the committees for several of these, almost always as treasurer. When he once protested that he should not be treasurer, as he had not even taken one course in bookkeeping or accounting, their response was "But you are honest." That was the only credential they sought.

In committing to 22 years of involvement in Costa Rica, we had to miss many family events, such as reunions at Christmastime, weddings of family siblings, and even family funerals. We were separated from our families by 4,000 miles. However, we were able to share in many special events with our brothers and sisters in the churches in Costa Rica, and they became our family. We were content.

The congregation in Sarapiquí in northern Costa Rica.

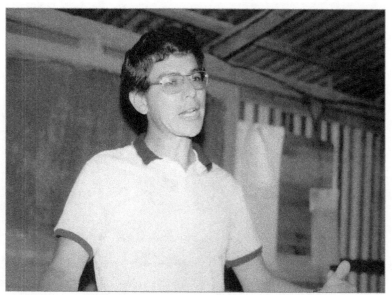

Orlando Carvajal, our first Costa Rican pastor.

The church in Talamanca in southeastern Costa Rica, The pastor,
Indalecio Molina, is playing the guitar.

Eileen teaching Christian education in Upala in
northwestern Costa Rica.

Official organization of the Costa Rica Mennonite Conference April, 1974.

*Recognition of Mark Peachey, our missions director from
Rosedale Mennonite Missions from 1961 to 1974.*

Chapter 9
TIME FOR TRANSITION

Elmer

As the churches and the Costa Rican Mennonite Conference developed and matured, Eileen and I learned to practice the flexibility that we were told we would need. Key positions were now in the hands of Costa Rican leaders and the church was moving forward.

I recall how good it felt after presiding the Costa Rican Mennonite Conference for six years, to now be able to sit back and enjoy seeing others take my place. There was no envy nor jealousy, nor reluctance to give up my position, nor thinking how much better I could do it. There was the joy of seeing others replace me as I released responsibility, and the assurance of knowing that the leadership of the church was in good hands. I was still given responsibilities as a counselor or mentor to local pastors.

Along with the changing of roles, our family was changing. Our older daughter Emily had graduated from high school in 1980, before we left for another visit to the United States. Emily began employment as a teaching assistant in a Christian school in our former home community in New York State. As we prepared to return to Costa Rica in early 1981, she asked to remain in New York State and continue working. She had been a part of two cultures, and felt she needed time to determine who she really was. Was she Costa Rican or North American? Many missionary children find they need to deal with this identity crisis.

Emily found that she was feeling more comfortable in North America, and as she worked under her supervisor, a single young man who had come from Ohio to work at the same school, a courtship developed and led to their marriage in June 1984.

Our second daughter Elnora graduated from high school in Costa Rica in 1981, enrolled at the same college in Virginia where we had graduated in 1960, and there met her husband-to-be who was from our former home community in New York State. They were married in August 1984. I performed the marriage ceremonies for both of our daughters, which were held at Lowville Mennonite Church, the same facility where Eileen and I were married 31 years earlier.

Our oldest son Erland soon became interested in graduating from the same Christian high school in Virginia where Eileen had graduated in 1949, so he moved into a dormitory there in 1982. It seemed like a good time for us to consider a leave of absence and be closer to our family.

Eileen and I decided that a two-year leave of absence would allow both of us to work on our Master's Degree, help our children get established, and allow the churches in Costa Rica to develop on their own. I had been the key leader for many years, and our absence for a couple of years would allow our churches

in Costa Rica to function without us, as they followed the leading of the Holy Spirit for future development.

Those of us who had held key positions in the church
needed to arrive at the place where we were willing to release
our responsibilities to others, step out of the way, and trust
the Holy Spirit to do His work through others. He knows
how to do that.

Thus, between 1980 and 1983, all of our family made the
move to the United States—one child each year and then four
of us in 1983. Family members helped us find a rented house
in Harrisonburg, Virginia, and we moved in June 1983. Our
twin sons, Marvin and Melvin enrolled at Eastern Mennonite High School, Eileen's alma mater. We made our church
home with New Covenant Mennonite Fellowship, an emerging congregation of a charismatic nature. After our years in
Costa Rica it seemed like a good fit. We were both involved
in some teaching and preaching, in a small group fellowship
and Elmer even served a term as elder. Our two sons were
involved in an active youth program.

Eileen had taken some graduate extension courses that were
offered through her teaching positions in Costa Rica, and now
our alma mater offered a Master of Education degree through
its graduate program. Courses were offered during the summer
months to persons who were employed during the school year.
Eileen was able to travel to the United States and study in Virginia for several weeks during two summers. After our move to
Virginia in 1983, she finished her course of study and received
her Master of Education degree. She then received employment
in the same Weekday Religious Education program for children
from grades three through five in public schools, where she had

taught for one year before we left for Costa Rica. This time she taught for three years, until our move to Ohio.

When Eileen taught 22 years earlier, the classes were held in the public schools. This time, to avoid legal challenges, the classes were held off campus, such as a nearby church or other facility that was available. The classes continued to be held during school hours on a released time basis. Many of the children were from unchurched families, and yet were given permission by their parents to attend the classes. Eileen travelled to four different schools for these one-hour-a week-classes. She was one of several teachers, all supported by local churches and individuals.

I returned to my seminary studies for the two more years that remained to complete my Master of Divinity degree. My first year of seminary studies had come 22 years earlier, right after college. As we returned to our studies in Virginia, we were now both past fifty years of age. However, study was not new. Our work had included extensive study over the years. But, now we were being told what to study. I found that a couple of my seminary professors were former college class-mates. They and I both enjoyed that relationship. I received my Master of Divinity degree from Eastern Mennonite Seminary in 1985.

Eileen and I expected to be in the United States for two years, and then return to Costa Rica for another long period, either until retirement or even including our retirement years. Those two years have now been extended to 33 years. True, we have returned to Costa Rica on many occasions since then, but only to visit. We have lived elsewhere since that time.

Some of those return visits were with the Choraleers, a musical group from Lancaster, Pennsylvania, under the leadership of my brother-in-law, Arnold Moshier. This group worked hard at singing in Spanish, even when they did not understand the words. They would give skits based directly on parables or miracles of Jesus, and we would both serve as their translators. The Choraleer ministry during its 40-year history under the leadership of my brother-in-law, made a huge impact upon our churches and their communities in Costa Rica, when they would usually visit for about a week at a time, and often on a yearly basis. Their visits began while we lived in Costa Rica and continued after we left. We would return to Costa Rica with them, giving us the opportunity to stay in touch with our churches there and the people we loved so much.

We anticipated a return to Costa Rica in 1985. Then, a surprise message came through from our mission agency headquarters. After contact with our church leaders in Costa Rica, they expressed deep appreciation for our years of ministry. But, they also expressed some doubts about the wisdom of our returning full-time. They had depended heavily upon us for leadership when we lived there, but now were learning to function without us. Yet, they did not want to lose us. Would there be an arrangement where we could be available for teaching and counsel, without direct involvement in the leadership of the churches?

At the same time, Rosedale Bible College, a two-year Bible College offering an Associate in Arts degree in Biblical Studies, was expanding its concentration of courses in mission studies and was asking Rosedale Mennonite Missions if they would have someone available to come and teach mission courses. The campus of Rosedale Bible College was located right beside the headquarters of Rosedale Mennonite Missions. Our mission agency was now suggesting that I teach during the school year and have summers available to minister in our churches in Latin America, not only Costa Rica, but also Nicaragua and Ecuador.

As we prayed and sought counsel, we sensed that this kind of arrangement seemed good to the church in Costa Rica, to Rosedale Mennonite Missions, to Rosedale Bible College, to the Lord, and to us. So, our next move fell into place, as we continued to practice stickability and flexibility. We would be moving to Ohio.

Chapter 10
OHIO, HERE WE COME

Eileen

Elmer and I wiped away the tears as we drove out of Harrisonburg, Virginia with our two automobiles and a rental truck, and said good-by to dear friends who generously helped us load up and move out. Elmer led the way in the rental truck, I followed in one vehicle, and our twin sons, Marvin and Melvin, completed the caravan in the other vehicle. They had decided to move with us and attend college in Columbus, Ohio.

Elmer had already taught for one year at Rosedale Bible College in the 1985-1986 school year while I stayed in Virginia and the twins finished high school. I continued in my third year of teaching Bible in the course called, "Weekday Religious Education" for the released time program in the public schools. Elmer would travel home every other weekend, and we soon decided one year of this was enough. Either we would move to Ohio as a family or we would return to Costa Rica. We moved to Ohio in June 1986.

We rented one of five apartments owned by Rosedale Mennonite Missions, which would be our temporary home until we made other arrangements. Our daughter Emily, with her husband, Conrad and their newborn son, had moved to Ohio to the same community. Our sons stayed with them for the summer while we spent several weeks in ministry in Costa Rica, Nicaragua, and Ecuador.

We knew that Elmer's job at Rosedale Bible College was waiting for him when we returned in August. I had an interview at a Christian school and was tentatively hired as an elementary teacher. However, when we returned to Ohio following our summer ministry in Latin America, I discovered that the school had decided they would not hire any new teachers. I was struck by the realization that I was unemployed. In the end, I received employment from a daycare center, which paid minimum wages, but it was a job.

Another issue was to decide on a home church among several in the area. We discovered that Shiloh Mennonite Church, located five miles from Rosedale Bible College, was making plans to plant a daughter church in the Hilliard community, a growing suburb on the northwest side of Columbus. The congregation was putting together a team of church planters who would be willing to move into the Hilliard community. Church planting excited us and we offered to be part of the team as it came together. We were at peace with this new arrangement of spending our winter months in Ohio, then going south to Latin America for the summer and returning in the fall. We did this for six successive summers from 1985 to 1990, spending ten or eleven weeks teaching short seminars, visiting churches and pastors, and equipping leaders. Those were sometimes long days, and we felt very useful and very used.

We decided Hilliard would be a good place to live, eighteen miles from Rosedale, and Elmer could commute in twenty-five minutes. We could be a part of the church planting team in Hilliard. There would be opportunity for me to find teaching employment in the growing Hilliard community, and it would be fairly easy for our two sons to commute to their college. We made contact with a Christian real estate agent, and decided on a house in Hilliard, which became our home for 28 years, longer than we have lived anywhere else.

Now we faced another issue. We had funds for a down payment but would need to get a loan. The first question the loan officer asked us was what loans we had now. We did not have any. What loans did we have in the past? The only money we had ever borrowed was from Elmer's father when in college, and that was an internal arrangement and did not give us any credit rating. Her next question was about credit cards. We had been overseas and did not have any credit cards. The loan officer had never faced a situation like this. Sitting in her office was a married couple that was 55 and 53 years old and had no credit rating. She did not give up hope.

We had lived in Harrisonburg, Virginia for three years. She told us to bring receipts from the electric and telephone companies showing we always paid our bills on time, and from our landlord showing we always paid our rent on time. "Also, bring a letter from our employer." Rosedale Mennonite Missions had been our employer for 25 years. Yes, the loan was approved, and it was not long until the mail brought more offers each week to try to convince us to accept credit cards. We ended up accepting two credit cards and have yet to pay any interest on them. We pay off the balance every month.

We moved to Hilliard in December 1986, into what would be our first owned home. I applied to the Hilliard City School District as a substitute teacher and was soon told I was the district's favorite. The full-time job never came, but I was hired in 1990 for four days a week as a Learning Disabilities tutor. I kept that position until my retirement in the year 2000.

A significant number of Spanish-speaking families had moved into the community and more kept coming. The children were learning English but there was a language barrier between their parents and their teachers. I was frequently called upon to serve as interpreter for the two parties to communicate. As I settled into one school, I became well acquainted with the regular teaching staff. Several of the teachers were Christians and invited me to attend an early weekly prayer time for the teachers who desired to attend, and sponsored by the teachers. On a number of occasions the principal of the school came to the meetings with special prayer requests. My ministry continued, even in the public school.

Rosedale Bible College was a two-year college, accredited to give an Associate in Arts Degree in Biblical Studies. Elmer taught several mission courses, including Introduction to Missions, Local Church Evangelism, Church Planting and Development, Church Leadership and Administration, Cultural Anthropology and Missionary Anthropology. He taught three New Testament courses, which were Pastoral Epistles, Prison Epistles, and the Book of Acts. He also taught Devotional Life. He did a one-time round of teaching: Introduction to World Religions; Composition; Congregational Worship and Music Leadership. He did not always teach full time, but he was on the faculty for a total of 18 years, all of this after 22 years in Costa Rica.

What about the church plant in Hilliard? We offered to assist but felt someone else would need to provide leadership because of our other responsibilities. A team of seven people came together, including two other young couples, and a single young man. All were enthusiastic youth, but saw us as the experienced church planters, so they looked to us to provide leadership, even though they were aware that we would be gone for several weeks each summer. These team members, and the mission board of the Shiloh Mennonite Church, confirmed this arrangement, so we accepted. We are convinced that the Lord does lead through the local church body.

Elmer served as the pastor for the first ten years, and then became the overseer as one of the other team members was installed as senior pastor. As pastor, he made it clear that this was a team ministry and we would all be involved in joint leadership with him as coordinator. All seven of us volunteered our time as we used the approach that was known as "planting churches on a shoe string." We officially began this outreach in September 1988. We agreed to name the church plant "Agape Community Fellowship." Today, 28 years later, the team concept continues. The job of the senior pastor was to serve as the coordinator of the team of four pastors and three elders. All share the pulpit ministry and other responsibilities in this congregation that numbers 150 – 175 in attendance. All of the leaders have other means of making a living.

Our assignment with Rosedale Mennonite Missions changed from spending ten or eleven weeks in Latin America each summer, as Elmer was named as director of Latin American Ministries for Rosedale Mennonite Missions in 1990. This was a part-time position as he continued to teach part-time at Rosedale Bible College.

We continued to travel to Costa Rica, Nicaragua, and Ecuador, but in more of an administrative role. Elmer's responsibilities also included oversight of emerging churches in San Antonio, Texas, Albuquerque, New Mexico, Phoenix, Arizona, and New York City. At all of these locations, work was being done among Hispanics. This role continued until 1994 when Elmer's assignment was again changed to work in Information Services at the home office. Yes, we knew by then what it meant to practice flexibility. We were relating to three different church entities, Rosedale Bible College, Rosedale Mennonite Missions, and Agape Community Fellowship. Our work included office responsibilities, the classroom, and pastoral leadership. God was making His plan clear to us through the body of believers. He knows the plan He has for us and His plan is always best. We can always feel secure when we risk our lives to His plan.

Our Hilliard home for 28 years, longer than we have lived anywhere else.

*Elmer ordaining Todd Waugh to the ministry at Pine Grove,
Castorland, New York.*

Elmer preaching as overseer, Lowville, New York.

Agape Community Fellowship, Hilliard, Ohio on a Sunday morning.

Chapter 11

THIS IS RETIREMENT

Elmer

Someone referred to retirement as climbing down the ladder. It helps if we can climb down gradually. Far too many people excitedly await their retirement day and getting to the list of activities they are going to accomplish. Then they finish the list in about three weeks and find life boring and meaningless after that. People need a reason to get up every morning.

For Eileen, retirement from teaching came at age 67 in the year 2000, at the end of the school year. She had taught at that school for ten years, and the principal arranged a farewell party for her. She sometimes crosses paths at the grocery store with former teachers but she has not been inside the school building since her day of her retirement.

We had both been volunteering a couple days per month at the Country Closet Thrift Shop since its opening in 1997. The Country Closet is one of more than 100 thrift shops in the United States and Canada that provide funding for the Mennonite Central Committee. This ministry of Mennonite Churches across North America ministers to material and relief needs around the world in the name of Christ. As soon as Eileen retired, the Board of Directors of the Country Closet asked her to become volunteer manager, and she served in this role for the next ten years, dedicating about 40% of her working hours to this role.

I retired more gradually; first from my part-time teaching position at Rosedale Bible College, and later from fifty percent employment to twenty-five percent employment at Rosedale Mennonite Missions, and finally to full-time retirement in 2006, after 45 years of serving with our mission agency. Both of us donated two days a week to the Country Closet, and then as we became octogenarians, we reduced our time to one day a week.

As we gradually phased into retirement, I was asked to serve as overseer to three congregations in 1998, including two local congregations in Ohio and one emerging congregation in Indiana. In 1999 the bishop who was the overseer of five congregations in our home community in New York State, decided that it was time to retire from that responsibility. Four more of those congregations asked me to serve as their overseer, for a total of seven. I filled this role of overseer for seven congregations for the next three years, and then gradually phased out over the next several years.

In the year 2001, after observing a steady increase in the number of Hispanics in the greater Columbus, Ohio community, Elam and Doris Stauffer contacted us. Did the Lord want us to be involved in reaching these Hispanics? They had served with Rosedale Mennonite Missions in Nicaragua and Ecuador and were now living in central Ohio. We invited two other couples to join us who had served in Latin America, as we launched a church planting ministry among the Hispanics of the area. In September 2001, we held our first Spanish-speaking service, held on a Sunday afternoon in the facility of Agape Community Fellowship.

David and Ana Villalta, a pastoral couple, was available in Costa Rica to serve the new congregation in Hilliard, Ohio. They arrived in August 2004 and I had ordained David to the ministry in Costa Rica in February 1983. We two original couples, who were instrumental in starting the congregation, served on the leadership team and assisted in teaching and preaching. I also served as the congregation's first treasurer. Eileen served for several years as the director of the children's Sunday school department.

What does one do in retirement? We joked that you continue to serve full time, but without getting paid. I also volunteer as a proofreader for publications of Rosedale Mennonite Missions and the Conservative Mennonite Conference. Thankfully, between retirement income and savings, we have been able to live comfortably, although not luxuriously. After living in our own home in Hilliard for 28 years, longer than anywhere else, we scaled down, sold our house, and moved three miles away to a condominium. This unit with two bedrooms, two baths, and a two-car garage, all on one floor, serves our needs well.

In more recent years we have been able to do some traveling. Some of it had to do with work responsibilities, such as teaching extension courses for Rosedale Bible College in Kenya, East Africa on two occasions. On a personal basis, we were able to visit Eileen's sister and husband in Egypt, where they directed an American school, and to visit another of Eileen's sisters and her husband who were assisting developing churches in Vietnam. We were able to take a tour to Europe and another to Alaska. On two occasions, we joined a vanload of relatives and friends to visit national parks in both northwest and southwest United States. In all, we have visited 42 of the 50 states of the United States, and 25 countries on five continents. What a blessed life it has been.

Having become octogenarians, health issues sometimes need special attention. I have had radiation for prostate cancer and Eileen has had surgery and radiation for a lump on her breast. I have had a pacemaker installed because of an irregular heartbeat. Eileen needs medication for arthritis and diabetes. Does this discourage us? Life continues to be meaningful and enjoyable as we are in our 80s and we thank God for a full and happy life and we continue to periodically return to Costa Rica and we rejoice to see the continued fruit of our labors.

To mention a few persons among many: Orlando, who arrived at church that first Sunday in 1963 as a barefoot 13-year-old boy, and in later years I performed his wedding ceremony and ordained him to the ministry. He continues in an active ministry.

On a recent visit to the Heredia congregation where we invested much time in earlier years, Eduardo moderated the service and was delighted to tell the congregation that I had performed his wedding ceremony 40 years ago.

Jaime Prieto's mother passed away when he was a child. Jaime was placed in a Christian children's home and then was given a home with one of the families of our Heredia congregation so that he could go to high school. Eventually, he studied in Europe in Heidelberg, Germany and received a Ph.D. He returned to Costa Rica to do seminary teaching, has authored a book on Mennonites in Latin America, and at present presides the Costa Rica Mennonite Conference.

Mario was converted at the end of his teenage years and was baptized at the Heredia church. He became an elementary teacher and taught for many years in the Sarapiqui community in northern Costa Rica where one of our congregations was located. Mario, now retired, saw several groups of believers emerge in small, somewhat isolated villages. He told me in more recent years that he does not remember any of my sermons but he remembers my life of consistency. Sometimes we preach our most powerful sermons not by our words, but by the way we live.

Anabelle was raised by her grandmother, lived for three years with one of our missionary families, and then worked for us for five years as she studied in night school and finished high school and then married. She and her husband attend the Heredia Mennonite Church and she replaced Eileen as Director of Christian Education. She has donated many hours to the Costa Rica Mennonite Conference in this role.

Jovita was one of our early believers and came to the Lord after a sad life of giving birth to ten children from three different men without being married to any of them. She eventually married the father of seven of those children, and she and her husband, Eladio made an outstanding contribution to the development of the congregation in Heredia. One time she commented that it was worth our going to Costa Rica just to minister to her. What a joy it is to look back and remember these persons, and many others, and know that our lives and ministry have made a difference.

Baptism at Iglesia Cristiana Hispana. Hilliard, Ohio.

David and Ana Villalta. David was ordained by Elmer in 1983 in Costa Rica. He served as pastor, then as president of the Costa Rica Mennonite Conference, then for thirteen years at Iglesia Cristiana Hispana in Hilliard, Ohio. They returned to Costa Rica in 2017 for retirement.

Elmer and Eileen with Jaime Prieto at Mennonite World Conference in Harrisburg, PA in 2015. Jaime is now the president of the Costa Rica Mennonite Conference.

The Country Closet Thrift Shop, where Elmer and Eileen volunteer one day per week. The thrift shop provides funds for the relief and service ministries of Mennonite Central Committee.

Chapter 12

YOU ARE OUR PORTION, O LORD

Everyone has a story. This has been our story. You have now received a glimpse into some of God's activity in our lives. We are amazed at how God could take two quite ordinary young people from two farm families in northern New York State, and blend our lives together in carrying out His beautiful purposes. As we have come to the sunset years of our lives, we look back with gratitude at how the Lord could use us. It was not because of our ability, but because of our availability. We have merely followed His lead, step by step.

This book has not been about some famous missionary heroes, but it is the story of how we have sought the Lord together, as He has shown us the way. It is about His faithfulness in going before us each step of the way.

Our story can be your story. We are not called to offer what we do not have. All of us can offer ourselves with what He has given us to the Lord of the Church. As stated previously, He will take our availability and enable us, equip us, empower us, and energize us. To Him be the glory in the Church and in His followers who are the Church and whom He uses to build His Church.

We conclude with the eight lessons we have learned in our missionary pilgrimage:

1. Our lives are influenced by others and we have an influence upon others. May that influence be a good one.

2. God leads us into responsibilities that are far too big for us but they are never too big for Him. He equips us and enables us, empowers us and energizes us, for the mission He has for us.

3. God gifts the church to minister. He does not want us to sit around and be smug about our spiritual gifts. He gifts us as a body to bless each other. We need the corporate body, the Church, as a discerning community.

4. To practice "flexibility and stickability." Those words spoken to us by our Missions Director in 1961 have proven to be true many times.

5. To wait upon the Lord. He is not always in a hurry but He is always on time. His timing is best.

6. To not be satisfied with merely doing well. Accept the best God has for you.

7. Decisions we make in life definitely impact what follows in later years.

8. God is dependable. We can risk our future to Him. Our security is in Him.

"You are my portion, O Lord. I have promised to obey your words." Psalm 119:57

Based on Psalm 119:57 in the King James Version of the Bible, below is our favorite hymn written by Isaac Watts in 1719. The hymn was included in the *Church Hymnal* published in 1927 by the Mennonite Publishing House of Scottdale, Pennsylvania and is reprinted here with the title "Thou Art My Portion."

Our complete family in 2013, the last time we were all together. Since then, a grandson-in-law, a granddaughter-in-law, and four great-grandchildren have been added to the family, for a total of 28 people.

Two recently married grandchildren with their spouses.

Our four great-grandchildren at Christmas, 2017.

Our present Condo home where we have moved in retirement.

CONCLUSION

During the years of working in this vineyard known as Costa Rica, Elmer and Eileen Lehman have impacted many lives. Sometimes they were used to plant the seed of the Gospel and were able to see that seed watered and grow to bear fruit. The following interviews reflect the impact they have made on the lives of three persons in their ministry in Costa Rica. Sometimes the reward is not seen on this earth. Sometimes God allows us to see the fruit that is born from the seeds planted by the power of the Gospel.

Lorena and Hilda are sisters and both were saved at the mission church in Costa Rica as children. Anabelle was also converted to Christ at a young age and shares her impression of the Lehmans and some of their insights regarding the impact of the Lehman family in their mission work in Heredia, Costa Rica.

Lorena

At the age of seven, Lorena was going through depression and did not want to live, as her brother, on a daily basis bullied her mercilessly at home. She recalls how on one December 24th, she and her mother were going downtown to buy a gift in the center of the city of Heredia. They heard the most beautiful music and her mother said, "Let's see where that music is coming from." They walked toward the mission church and found Elmer behind the pulpit leading the song, "You Left Your Throne and Crown for Me."

As Lorena listened to the song, she heard the words, "I want a place to rest but there is no place to rest." She said to God, "You can rest in my heart." She lifted her hands and wept. When Elmer asked who wanted to accept Jesus, she and her mother lifted their hands. She felt that Elmer and Eileen, perhaps, did not think she was serious because she was so young. Perhaps they thought she did not understand, but she knew she wanted Jesus.

Lorena's sadness and depression left and a light came into her heart. Her mother told her not to tell anyone where they had been, but she went home and told her sister Hilda to ask Jesus into her heart. Hilda threatened to tell their father because they were not supposed to talk about these things as Catholics. From the day she and her mother accepted Jesus opposition was strong. The extended family disowned them, but no one told their secret to their father. She and her mother went to Sunday school the next week.

Innocently, after returning from church, Lorena showed her father her coloring sheet and that is when he knew. He was angry and burned her mother's Bible. He declared that there would be no traitors in his house. Going against the Catholic faith was very treacherous.

For a time they were forbidden to go back to the mission church and Lorena cried a lot. With time, her mother led all the children to Christ and they prayed for their father. Every time her mother acquired a Bible, he would burn it, so they would sing the songs they learned at the mission church. One day he decided to prove that her Bible was false and the Catholic Bible was real. For one year they sat and compared Bibles at home. Then one night her father told her mother, "I want to go to church with you." He was saved and a turn-around was made for the family.

Lorena reflected that she was amazed at how Elmer and Eileen Lehman came from another country, to Costa Rica, to bring the Good News that changed the whole family. The greatest impact that they made on her life was from the love they gave to her.

Lorena told of one day when everyone in the family was sick. They had no food and no clean clothes. They were so embarrassed and too poor for vaccinations and within their family they had a variety of illnesses at the time, including chickenpox, measles, and whooping cough. Death was everywhere—dirty clothes were everywhere. They should have been dead, as sheets were full of blood, but Elmer and Eileen came with such love. They came with trays of food and instead of making them feel gross, Eileen washed the laundry without disdain and fear of getting sick herself.

This memory serves as the foundation of her feelings for them. When asked to describe in one word her feelings for the Lehman's, she used two words: Spiritual Parents. She noted that it is a pleasure and an honor to have this blessing she has received through their lives and ministry, and she loves and blesses them.

Hilda

"I was not home when they received Christ."

Hilda reflected on the changes that were made while she was away in a remote place working for a family for three months. She was sent away more than once and this time she was feeling isolated and rejected. Her relationship with her mother previously involved physical abuse. This time when she returned home, her mother took her shopping.

Hilda recognized the song that Lorena had told her about. Her mother asked her, "Do you hear the song?" She said, "Yes." The music was captivating and they walked to the chapel. The first person Hilda saw was Elmer. To her, he was the most wonderful and beautiful human being because his voice was so wonderful. When he said, "Raise your hand if you want to accept Jesus," she wanted to lift her hand so badly. But, her mother made her raise her hand, and it turned her away from making a true decision in her heart. This happened over and over, every time she went to the church. She would be moved to accept Christ, but then her mother would nudge her and say, "Raise your hand." She would do it out of obligation, but with anger rather than sweet surrender.

Finally, when Hilda was eleven, she decided that she would give her heart to Christ at a crusade that was coming to town. Unfortunately, her mother went with her and again tried to obligate her. Finally, one day her mother missed church.

Eileen had a gift for teaching, and every Sunday morning Hilda tried not to miss her class. The Sunday her mother was absent, Hilda lifted her hand in the class in response to the invitation to receive Jesus. This time she meant it! Before taking that step, she was so sad that she asked God to let her die. She meant it because of the loneliness she felt. Her experience in giving her life to Jesus was so amazing because she felt Jesus behind her and could feel His hand on her shoulder, covering her. Four desires sprang in her heart the day she received Jesus. First, she wanted to go back to school. She had to drop out when she was in the fourth grade. Second, she wanted to go to high school. Third, she wanted to have her own Bible. They had no money to buy one. Fourth, her most important wish was to be a nurse. Through God's grace, all of her desires were met.

The impact that Elmer and Eileen Lehman had on Hilda's life was great, through their mission work in Costa Rica. The mission church was like her second home. The services were very important to her and she was left with an impact that she still carries today regarding the importance of church fellowship. Through the ministry of patience, acceptance, and love that she felt from Elmer, she was injected with that same type of care and concern for others. They included her in everything their children did. Eileen left a legacy of teaching to her and it has served as a foundation for her love of the Word. She was starved to receive teaching about Jesus and to this day she has a passion for it and discipleship.

The word Hilda used to describe what she feels for Elmer and Eileen Lehman is respect. She is thankful for their lives and sacrifices, and for what they sowed into her. They left a great, godly example and she hopes to be able to give the way they did.

Anabelle

There are a few persons who accepted Christ as children that are still serving at the church that Elmer and Eileen Lehman started many years ago. Anabelle is one of them.

Anabelle was eleven years old and living in Heredia with her cousins who were going to a church different from the one she attended. She had been going with her grandmother to a Seventh Day Adventist Church. Her aunt invited her to go with their children to the church Elmer and Eileen Lehman presided over. Eileen was teaching Sunday school and Anabelle remembers listening intently those first two weeks.

Anabelle accepted Christ one Sunday after Eileen presented the Gospel. She remembers that the Adventist Church was focused on rules and that Jesus forgave them when they broke the rules. She invited her grandmother to go with her to church so she could eat pork in pork tamales and have coffee. These were things her grandmother loved but had given them up because of the rules of her church. Her grandmother went with her and that was it.

Anabelle was baptized at age twelve and decided she wanted to teach Sunday school to the children. She wanted to teach them to follow Jesus and not rules. She started teaching Sunday school at age thirteen with Eileen's help. She even started helping in the church before this by taking up the offering in a basket every Sunday.

Anabelle stopped going out with friends so that she could be faithful to her church assignment. At that time, the attendance at the church was only between 13 and 25 people. She was one of the first members and remembers being saved along with Hilda and being baptized along with her.

"Elmer and Eileen had such a compassionate way about them." She remembers her cousin Orlando saying, "I don't remember what they said to me. But I remember them kindly touching my head and looking me in the eyes." They made each child feel valued and invited them to eat and play and make crafts.

Anabelle remembers doing fundraisers twice a year for the church, especially in December when people had more money. They would sell clothes, crafts, candles, and tamales.

The greatest impact Elmer and Eileen had on her life was when they adopted twin sons and she started working for them. The babies were not well and she felt a need to help care for them. She loved them very much. Thankfully, they recovered. The impact of living out evangelism in works, and not just words, made a lasting impact upon her.

Elmer and Eileen were also very instrumental in helping her make decisions for her future. She and her grandmother moved onto the church property while she attended night school and worked for Eileen and cared for the twins. She worked for them for six years. After high school they encouraged her to do a term of voluntary service along with her cousin Orlando. These opportunities set the course for her to serve the Lord the rest of her life.

These connections and relationships are still strong today. The Lehmans helped her plan her wedding and Elmer performed the marriage ceremony. Anabelle continues, to this day, to organize a Vacation Bible school for children like she used to help Eileen with as a youth. As she describes Elmer and Eileen, she could think of no better description than "Walking Servants."

Anabelle watched Elmer and Eileen work outside of their church in organizations that helped people to learn to read, going into people's homes to do personal Bible studies, helping establish churches in other parts of Costa Rica, exemplifying true evangelism and discipleship in what is now widely known as "church planting." Anabelle considers it an honor to be a part of their legacy.

Lorena and Hilda with their younger sister Rosa.

Anabelle with her dear friend and mentor Eileen.

ABOUT THE AUTHORS

Elmer and Eileen Lehman grew up on dairy farms in rural northern New York State. Following their marriage, they administered a children's home for two years in Mennonite Voluntary Service in Puerto Rico. This was followed by academic preparation and twenty-two years as missionaries in Costa Rica. In later years they moved to Ohio where Elmer taught at Rosedale Bible College and worked in the offices of Rosedale Mennonite Missions. Eileen worked as a Learning Disabilities tutor in the Hilliard, Ohio school district. They were part of a church planting team to begin Agape Community Fellowship in Hilliard in 1988. Elmer served as senior pastor for the first ten years and then as overseer. They were part of a church planting team to begin a Spanish-speaking congregation, Iglesia Cristiana Hispana in 2001. After retirement, Eileen gave ten years as volunteer manager of the Country Closet Thrift Shop, a ministry of relief and service sponsored by the Mennonite Central Committee. Elmer and Eileen continue to serve as volunteers at the Country Closet Thrift Shop and assist in the ministry of a Spanish-speaking congregation, the Iglesia Cristiana Hispana. They live in Hilliard, Ohio, are the parents of five children, nine grandchildren, and four great-grandchildren.

The Lehman's would love to hear from you!

Elmer and Eileen Lehman

2594 Roberts Court

Hilliard, OH 43026

E-mail: elmereileen@gmail.com

Morgan James
Speakers Group

www.TheMorganJamesSpeakersGroup.com

We connect Morgan James published
authors with live and online events
and audiences who will benefit
from their expertise.

Printed in the USA
CPSIA information can be obtained
at www.ICGtesting.com
JSHW082353140824
68134JS00020B/2063

9 781683 508953